Surviving Crippling Poverty
Tadhg O'Flaherty

Copyright © 2017 by Tadhg O'Flaherty

All Rights Reserved. No part of this publication may be reproduced, distributed, or transmitted in any form or by any means, including photocopying, recording, or other electronic or mechanical methods, without the prior written permission of the author, except in the case of brief quotations embodied in critical reviews and certain other noncommercial uses permitted by copyright law.

This document provides exact and reliable information with regards to the topic covered. The publication is sold under the understanding that the author is not required to render accounting, officially permitted, or otherwise, qualified services. If further advice is required, legal or professional, a practised individual in the required profession should be consulted.

The information contained in this book is intended for educational purposes only and is not for diagnosis, prescription or treatment of any health disorder whatsoever. The techniques described within should not be performed without first consulting with a competent health care or legal professional and/or a professional within the respective field. By following the various techniques described in this book you do so at your own risk.

The author will not be held liable for any reparation, damages, or monetary loss due to the use or misuse of the material contained within. The information within is offered for informational purposes only and is without contract or any type of guarantee.

ISBN-13: 978-1-52058-394-5

To the cripplingly poor.

You will pull through this.

You will survive.

You will thrive.

Table of Contents

Introduction 1

ACT NOW! 3

   Calculating your wealth 4

   Help 7

   Stop planning for the future 8

Entertainment 11

   TV 12

   Cinema 14

   Restaurants 16

   Drinking 17

   Parties 18

   Stop splitting the bill 20

   Free entertainment 21

Food 24

   Grow your own food 27

   Stews and soups 35

   Urban farm animals 37

   Potluck dinner bonanza 40

   Farmers markets 42

   Importance of the shopping list 44

   Buying food in bulk 46

- Free condiments 49
- The power of positive thinking 51
  - Gratitude 53
  - Staying grounded 55
  - Taking intuitive action 57
- Expensive vices 59
  - 24-hour purchasing rule 61
  - Lasting purchases 63
- Pets 66
- Special occasions and gift giving 69
  - Homemade crafts 71
- Making extra money 75
  - Cutting lawns 76
  - Washing cars 77
  - Dog walker 79
  - Recycle for cash 80
  - Stay out of trouble 82
  - Grab hold of opportunities 84
- Cashing in 86
  - Downgrading 88
  - Do you really need those 90
- Second-hand stores 94

- Always dress well 96
- Dumpster diving 98
- Coupons 100
- Utility bills 103
  - Cheaper electricity 106
- Banking 110
  - Stop investing in banks 112
  - Stop all automatic debits 114
  - Pay-day loans 115
  - Credit cards 118
- Healthcare 121
  - Go outside 123
  - Exercise 125
  - Meditation 127
- Employment costs money 129
- Preparing for the worst 131
  - Join a local church 133
  - Find emergency services 135
  - Living in your car 137
  - Dangers of homelessness 140
  - Shoplifting 142
- A brighter future? 144

Never give up...146
Remember to give back 148
Conclusion..150

Introduction

"There are people in the world so hungry, that God cannot appear to them except in the form of bread."
Mahatma Gandhi (1869-1948)

Ever since the financial crash of 2008 hundreds of millions of people around the world have gone poor, with many of them losing everything, from their vast savings accounts to the ability for supplying basic necessities for them and their family.

By taking immediate action and making sweeping changes to your way of life it can be possible to save your home and maintain a basic level of existence. Crippling poverty is usually a temporary situation that can change for the better. Most people who become poor do not end up living on the streets and some manage to come out the other end of crippling poverty with their own fledgeling business that grows by leaps and bounds.

Surviving with little or no money is possible with many people doing just that on a daily basis. By reading this book you are taking the first steps to correcting your financial situation and gaining control over your spending. Accept that things have now changed and begin working towards a far cheaper and more economical future.

ACT NOW!

"Take time to deliberate; but when the time for action arrives, stop thinking and go in."
Andrew Jackson (1767-1845)

Don't wait! The moment you lose your job or the moment that first threatening letter from the credit card company arrives on your doorstep you will need to take immediate and drastic action to get your finances back in shape. You are reading this book for a very good reason. Even if you are in full-time employment it is still possible to fall into the trap of crippling poverty.

You may have large amounts of money stashed away in a savings account, for this very occasion, but this can vanish extremely quickly if you continue to maintain a spendthrift lifestyle. By applying the techniques presented in this book it can reduce your spending by potentially a large amount. The lower your weekly outlay of cash the longer you will be able to survive. It is time to make some radical changes in your current lifestyle, which may seem harsh at first but can be done while maintaining a fairly good standard of life.

As you read each section, take the information contained to heart and begin making changes. Remember, your savings account is for emergencies, just like the one you now face, but if you can keep as much money in there as possible it will ensure that you survive for far longer. After all... when it's gone, it's gone.

Calculating your wealth

"Don't gain the world & lose your soul, wisdom is better than Silver or Gold."
Bob Marley (1945-1981)

People have a tendency to interchange the words wealthy and rich without truly knowing the difference between the two.

When you are rich you have a lot of money coming in, you have affluence and plenty of spending power. You may have a very high income, you may even have tens of thousands of euro coming in every month, but this does not make you wealthy. There are plenty of people who are extremely rich who went broke overnight.

Let's take the example of a high-flying Wall Street executive who is making €10,000 per month. Due to such a vast income he enjoys a fantastic life, he buys plenty of things, he enjoys nights out on the town and he spends every single cent of that €10,000, every month. In this scenario, that Wall Street banker is exceedingly rich but he is not wealthy at all.

As opposed to riches, which is calculated as an amount of money, wealth is calculated as an amount of time. Your wealth is based on how much time you can survive if your income ended today, while you continue to enjoy the same lifestyle. Our Wall Street banker has a wealth of zero days because he spends all of the money that he earns. If he had managed to save just one month's wages then he's wealth would have been one month because he could continue to fund his current lifestyle for that length of time.

It is important to calculate your wealth. Spend some time today to sit down and go over all of your expenses. Account for everything, not just utility bills for also your weekly date night, all of those cups of coffee you have while at work, the cost of fuel... everything.

Once you have calculated your total monthly expenditure simply divide your savings by this amount. This will tell you how wealthy you are. Let's say you have a total expenditure of €1,000 per month and you have €5,000 in your savings account. Based on these figures you have a wealth of 5 months.

It is important, no matter how poor you are, to always try and maintain a wealth of at least one month. If you find that your wealth calculation is anywhere under 3 months it is time to dramatically cut your expenses and lifestyle immediately. When it comes to finances, wealth is the most important figure. It is more important than your nights out on the town, than your big car, and then you're huge house or buying the latest items.

Help

"Ask for help not because you're weak, but because you want to remain strong."
Les Brown (1945-)

Asking for help, even from family and friends can be a very painful and shame-inducing experience. Most people, when faced with the prospect of crippling poverty will actually shy away from seeking out any form of help or assistance. Stigmas associated with poverty run deep in today's culture and this sense of shame is very difficult to overcome.

While family and friends can help by giving you money, this will not be enough to fully sustain you over the long-run. Look for other avenues of help from those close to you in the form of meals or odd jobs around their homes for cash. People would rather pay someone they know well, rather than a professional stranger, when it comes to maintenance work on their home.

Most countries provide a social welfare system where you are paid a basic subsistence while unemployed or chronically poor. Visit your local social welfare office to determine what your current entitlements may be. This small amount of money each week may mean that you can save your home, or car, or simply put food on the table.

Stop planning for the future

> *"Tomorrow is tomorrow.*
> *Future cares have future cures,*
> *And we must mind today."*
> Sophocles (c. 498-406 BC)

If your wealth is drastically bad you need to stop all plans that you've made for the future. If you have purchased flight tickets for a holiday it's time to start cancelling them, if you have already secured a huge mortgage on a new house, but haven't finalised the sale yet, it's time to go to the bank and put a stop to that. All of your plans for the future are now gone and you must plan for right now... today only.

Create a list of household priorities. This list should include:

- Water
- Food
- Clothing
- Heating
- Electricity

The list can be as long as you like, provided that it only includes those items which are necessary for daily survival. Calculate the minimum amount of money required per month for each item.

Create a second list which includes every single item that you spend money on right now, add up the total and compare this to your current monthly income. If your monthly expenditures are higher than your monthly income it is time to cut back everything to the first list, the most basic survival expenditure.

Should you find that the money spent on everything is extremely close to your monthly income, but doesn't allow for anything left over, you could half the cost of everything on that list to see if this would be an acceptable living standard until things change for the better. Are you able to live on half the food you normally eat or can you downgrade the satellite TV package?

Your poverty may be a temporary situation or it may last for quite a long time. Regardless of how much money you may have right now or regardless of your current income, it is important to stretch out your finances for as long as possible. This will ensure that your wealth remains for as long as it possibly can.

These future plans will also include any recurring upcoming entertainment expenditure such as cable TV, a planned trip to the cinema with friends or that cruise planned for 3 years from now. Don't assume that your financial situation will have improved in the coming years. If it is not in a good condition now it could potentially take months or even years to fully recover.

Entertainment

"I find television very educating. Every time somebody turns on the set, I go into the other room and read a book."
Groucho Marx (1890-1977)

We all need to be entertained, but this need can lead to a lot of wasted money. The amount of money spent on entertainment varies from country, social class and whether or not you live in the city or country.

Entertainment expenses can mount up very quickly so these should be the things that are curtailed first when facing a financial crisis. Many entertainment vices are completely overlooked, such as TV subscription, when calculating expenses or they are classified as vital necessities. It can, of course, be argued that a monthly TV subscription should be kept, especially if you are going to dramatically reduce, or cut out, other forms of entertainment, yet it is possible to get even this basic entertainment for completely free.

There is more than enough ways to entertain yourself without spending any money or far cheaper ways than you thought. The savings made from cutting entertainment expenses are badly needed now in order to just survive. Once your finances return to normal you can always begin spending money on entertainment if you wish.

TV

That satellite subscription you have, you know the one… it has several thousand channels with every sport imaginable and more movie channels than every cinema in the country. Yea, that one! It needs to go and should be cancelled immediately. Check your contract to see if it includes a cancellation fee or other restrictive financial burden which may be imposed if you were to stop your subscription early.

Don't worry about the missed movies, sporting events or mindless reality garbage as almost all of it is freely available. If you have a terrestrial or broadcast digital TV system entering your home it can be accessed free of charge (no monthly subscription). In the case of a terrestrial signal you may only need to have a UHF aerial on the roof of your home; however, a digital TV signal will require a decoder box. These boxes can range from €50-€200 but are a once-off charge and will still represent significant savings when compared to a monthly subscription to satellite TV. Approximately 95% of the shows you regularly watch on satellite TV are still available on free-to-air channels.

The internet is filled with streams of your favourite TV shows and movies. While it is completely illegal in most countries to download movies or TV shows, there is nothing illegal about streaming these shows. Streaming means that you watch the video on a web browser. The difference is that the company or individual responsible for the stream is the one who is breaking the law, just because you are watching the video online does not mean that you intentionally steal the video (by downloading) so that you can watch it later.

Search the internet to see how others have created free TV systems with freely available software solutions and online streaming. It can be easily accomplished in such a way that your new online system becomes far better than the expensive satellite TV subscription.

Cinema

Now that you have your new online TV system set up and running smoothly it is time to become creative with your weekly cinema trips. Such trips, while still far cheaper than a night out, can still incur large expenses, especially now that you are poor.

It might sound corny but setting up a series or blankets around the TV, with the lights dimmed can create a cinema-like experience. If this becomes a once per week event, just setting up those blankets will get you into the mindset of having a night at the movies.

Restrict your movie watching, as a general rule, to no more than 1 movie per night. If you sit around all day just watching TV or movies then how can your cinema night seem special? Restricting your TV time will also allow you to focus on more important things, like making money, paying off your debts, or exercising.

To save money on expensive concessions you could make popcorn at home or keep a stash of cheap, yet cheerful, sweets on hand. The most important thing to remember is to not eat all of those sweets before cinema night. Remain strong and keep sweets for special occasions. Expensive sodas could be replaced with flavoured water or homemade juice.

I know you really want to have the atmosphere, lights and sounds of the big screen but you need to save money. A weekly cinema night, in an actual cinema, can always be scheduled again once your finances return to normal.

Restaurants

Restaurants can be some of the most expensive forms of entertainment for people suffering from a financial crisis. You may have become accustomed to frequenting a fancy restaurant once a week or once per month at a cost of maybe €100 per trip. This equates to €5,200 or €1,200 per year, depending on how often you eat out. Even if you just went once per month, €1,200 could be used for far more important things such as:

- Home insurance
- Holidays & special occasions
- Car payments
- Mortgage or rent payments

While monthly meals out can be a very enjoyable experience it does not need to cost a small fortune. The first step is to sit down and calculate how often you eat out and how much it could be costing you. If you determine that you frequent restaurants once per month, cut this in half and only eat out once every 2 months. Search your local area for a far cheaper alternative to the expensive place you used to go. If you can find a place that offers a meal deal for €14.99 and you are paying for yourself and a significant other, whilst only eating out once every 2 months, your yearly restaurant expenses will drop from €1,200 per year to only €179.88. Saving over €1,000 per year can, and will, go a long way to restoring your financial situation.

Drinking

You don't need to have wild nights out. It is possible to return home, completely sober and still have an enjoyable time. Sound crazy? It is more than possible. When meeting friends for a night out drive into town. This will ensure that you are not allowed to drink so are restricted to sodas and soft drinks only. For the first few times, it will be difficult to stay strong but keep in mind that a drink driving charge can set your finances back by a very large amount.

Instead of spending long hours in the pub, it is acceptable to leave before midnight. You will wake up without a hangover and be able to accomplish a lot more the following day than your friends. There is no worse feeling, for those of us that are poor, then waking up with a bad hangover and an empty wallet. It can mean the difference between eating or not. This huge chunk of missing money could mean that you don't put the heating on for a week or more.

Don't worry about what your friends may think of this. If they are true friends they will understand. An acceptable lie, should you find it too embarrassing to tell them you're poor, is to say that you've given up drinking in order to live healthier.

Parties

If you are used to being the host or hostess and threw lavish parties at your home, maybe once a week or once per month, it is time to put an immediate stop to this activity. When you host a party it will inevitably cost you a small fortune and could also result in broken furniture, glasses, ornaments or electronic items from drunken party guests falling into them. Broken things were once easily replaced but this is a time to look after and value your possessions.

Feel free to attend as many parties as you like, just don't spend a lot of money doing this. Another thing to keep in mind is that your friends will, at some stage, expect you to reciprocate if you continue to enjoy their parties.

One of the best kinds of party to throw at your own house is a poker night/potluck dinner. All you need is a deck of cards, some poker chips and a cheap dish of your own creating. Every guest must bring their own drink and a dish for the potluck element of the evening. Never bet for real money, no matter how much pressure your friends apply because the chances of winning are very small. If pressure is being applied, play several hands for chips only and then step away from the game while your friends play for real money.

Stop splitting the bill

You might be used to nights out with friends or meals in fancy restaurants with family but these days are gone. Now that you are poor it is important to dramatically cut back all spending, even if that means sacrificing social interactions and entertainment. No, you don't have to hide away and become a social pariah. Going out with family and friends is still possible as long as you immediately stop splitting the bill.

It is easy to assume that those around us are living with the same limited resources that we have, or that they will suddenly alter their own spending behaviour to suit your new poverty status, but this is never the case. The people around you will continue to order the €25 steak and bottle of wine while you hungrily enjoy a cheap salad and only drink water. When it comes time to deal with the bill they will happily suggest splitting it, like always. When going for a meal or night out make sure you state clearly that you are going it alone and paying for your own food. Be sure to tell the waiter and stick to your guns. It doesn't matter how long you have been splitting the bill for, it all stops now.

The same applies when going to the pub for a night out. Stay as far away from doing rounds as possible. As with the meal, explain to your friends that you are buying your own drinks and not engaging in rounds. If questioned about this just tell them you are poor now. True friends will understand and leave you out of the rounds system from now on. Just because they are guzzling back drinks like there's no tomorrow, does not mean you have to. Enjoy a few drinks and go home early. The more you drink, the more you will want to drink so stay calm when out in the pub.

Free entertainment

While it may seem like there is nothing to do, when you are poor, there are actually plenty of opportunities to enjoy new experiences and entertainment completely free.

Most large cities have free museums which are usually massive. In this case, a single museum could account for an entire day trip. Take things slowly and see as much as you possibly can. Even those museums that charge an entry fee sometimes run a free night to promote a new collection or a new building extension. Some art galleries are free to visit with university campus's offering the largest collection for free events each year.

If you volunteer to assist at concerts or a community event this will usually include free entry or, if you are still volunteering while the event is on, it can be enjoyed. You will meet a lot of people while volunteering and not all of them are in the same poverty-stricken condition as yourself. Some very rich people volunteer as a way of giving back to their community and this can present a great opportunity to find a job or open you to, otherwise unseen, opportunities.

Some areas will have free movie nights, bands playing in the park, or on a pier, etc. Take advantage of these free entertainment opportunities as frequently as possible.

Even if it's something you know you won't enjoy it may provide a new perspective and could be something enjoyable if you just give it a chance.

Visit every park or outdoor recreational area near you and take the time to enjoy a picnic or two. If you enjoy travelling bring a tent and rough it. This will provide you with the ability to enjoy holidays as cheaply as possible.

Some cities allow you to participate in street sports events such as marathons or fun runs for free or for a nominal fee. These events could quickly turn into an enjoyable day out and don't need to cost a lot. There is never a reason to feel bored, or too poor to enjoy yourself. This world is filled to overflowing with things to see and do, just figure out how to do it all for free.

Food

"You don't need a silver fork to eat good food."
Paul Prudhomme (1940-2015)

By far the most expensive, yet vitally necessary item to purchase on a continuous basis is food. You simply cannot survive without it and will die from starvation if you go without food for 30-40 days. It is time to rethink your purchasing choices when it comes to food. If in the past, you have enjoyed organic produce from the local health-food store you will need to scale this exorbitant spending to large scale, and cheap, grocery stores.

When deciding to change spending habits concerning food, first calculate all of your finances. Maybe a downgrade of home or car could fix the problem just enough for you to maintain your current food budget. Food is very important, but good nutritious food is also very important. It is impossible to survive over a long period of time on potato chips or chocolate. If however, you find that your current monthly food expenses will clean out the savings account within a few months you will need to abandon nutrition and change food habits to less desirable food types.

When shopping in the supermarket always check the bargain bucket first, as there can be some great savings made here. Most of these items will be reduced in price due to small imperfections in the packaging or shape, rather than for being gone-off. Most large stores also offer free samples, either on promotional stalls or in the fresh produce section. Take full advantage of these free samples and eat as much as you can get away with.

The most expensive products are usually stacked at eye level. Always remember this when browsing the shelves and get into the habit of checking items on the top shelf or lower shelf. What you will find is similar items, of an unknown brand, being offered for up to half the price of the named brand items at eye level. Plenty of money and research has gone into ensuring that people will buy those items that produce the most profit for the store, which includes things like, placing expensive items at eye level or ensuring that small, seemingly inexpensive items are placed by the till to ensure impulse buys.

Be on the alert when grocery shopping and if you find yourself selecting any product based on what you normally would select, or if others are selecting the same product it is time to slow down and take a much closer look at how you are shopping. It could be that the psychological ploys of the grocery store are dictating your decisions. Step back and search for every variant of the product you were about to purchase to see if there is a cheaper version nearby.

The final tip, when it comes to grocery shopping, is to always stick to your shopping list and **never shop for food while you are hungry**, as this will drastically impact your decision making.

Grow your own food

Did you know that 83% of the space in an average back garden, in an urban environment, goes unused? You bought this space along with your house and you are doing nothing with it. Why not build your own food garden filled with fruits and vegetables. It is surprisingly easy to begin growing your own food in your back garden.

It may seem counter-intuitive to invest in gardening equipment, seeds or plants while you are poor, but this is actually the best time and it does not cost a lot to get started. This does not need to be a muddy or messy process with many backyard farmers opting for individual wooden planters that can grow several crops at a time. Each wooden planter can be divided by a small walkway giving you access to each of your crops. These wooden planters can be purchased, scavenged or even built cheaply if you are any good with tools and basic construction.

Even if you can grow enough food to feed 1 person in your family for a year it can significantly reduce your household bills. Before you begin it is important to identify the fruits and vegetables that you enjoy eating and the ones that you would tolerate eating. Once you have decided on a list of crops get yourself to the library or search the internet to determine if those crops will grow successfully in your country or region as not all foods can be grown everywhere, it would be heavily dependent on your climate and soil conditions.

When growing your own food it may be beneficial, depending on the particular crop, if you stagger the planting as this will result in a staggered harvest over a period of time. Let's say that you plant potatoes over a period of 4 weeks (if possible). When it comes time to harvest them you do not need to gather so many potatoes that it becomes impossible to eat them all or store them. You will harvest these potatoes once a week for 4 weeks which will result in far less wastage.

Below is a sample list of crops, which are extremely easy to grow and harvest. A planting calendar is available free from my website, www.tadhgfla.com/subscribe/ which shows the best times to plant and harvest various crops.

In most instances, the only things needed to get started are soil and seeds. These seeds can be purchased from almost any hardware or DIY store and come in small packets ready for planting.

Potatoes

<u>Benefits:</u> Potatoes are considered the number 1 vegetable in the world and are high in vitamins B3, B6 and C, potassium, manganese, fibre, copper, niacin and phosphorous.

<u>Growing:</u> Potatoes require a cool climate to grow but have the potential to be grown during the winter months in warmer climates. Cut a regular potato in half and leave to settle for 2 days before planting. Potatoes should be planted 30cm (1 foot) apart and 10cm (4 inches) deep. Spread manure in the bottom of each planting hole before placing the potato.

Harvest: Potatoes will take approximately 10 weeks to grow and should be removed from the soil very carefully. If you notice that the plants have died before the 10-week growing time take immediate action and harvest the entire crop. Most of the potatoes will have survived. Remove all loose mud and soil from the potatoes and store in a cool dark place, such as a closed cupboard.

Peas

Benefits: Peas are high in iron, fibre, potassium and vitamins A and C.

Growing: Plant peas about 25.5cm (10 inches) deep and leave approximately 5cm (2 inches) between each pea. Put bamboo stakes into the soil for each pea to climb up. Peas require plenty of water.

Harvest: Plant in early spring and again in late summer. Peas take between 12 and 16 weeks to mature. Peas should be harvested when the pods begin to fatten and before the peas get too big and split the pod.

Carrots

<u>Benefits:</u> Carrots are high in potassium, vitamins A, B6, and C, niacin, fibre and magnesium.

<u>Growing:</u> Carrot seeds should be kept at least 7.5cm (3 inches) apart and should be buried 30.5cm (12 inches) deep.

<u>Harvest:</u> Don't allow carrots to get too large. They taste better if harvested when small, about 1.3cm (0.5 inches) in diameter. Carrots should be ready to harvest after about 2 months. Simply pull them out of the ground and cut off the green stem before storing.

Lettuce

<u>Benefits:</u> Lettuce has very large water content and is high in protein, calcium and vitamins A, C and K.

<u>Growing:</u> Plant lettuce in early spring and again in autumn. The soil should be prepared by adding manure 1 week before planting and seeds should be at a depth of

1.3cm (0.5 inches) and 15.25cm (6 inches) apart and water generously at the time of planting.

Harvest: Lettuce takes between 45 and 55 days to grow. You do not need to fully remove the head of lettuce and can just take the outer leaves. This allows the plant to continue growing, thus providing, even more, lettuce. Once you have extracted enough leaves you can cut the head of lettuce from the root and leave the root in place. This can result in a second growing period occurring.

Tomatoes

Benefits: Tomatoes are high in fibre, vitamins A, B6 and C, potassium, magnesium, iron and lycopene.

Growing: Plant tomato seeds in indoor planters approximately 8 weeks before late spring. After this 8 week period transplant the seedlings into the garden. Ensure that the area selected for planting receives direct sunlight for most of the day. Manure should be added to the soil, in your garden, approximately 1 week before planting the seedlings outdoors. Bamboo stakes should be supplied for the plants to climb and each seedling should be spaced 0.6 metres (2 feet) apart. Give a generous amount of water at the time of transplanting.

Harvest: Tomatoes take 6 to 8 weeks to fully mature. As soon as a tomato looks very red in colour and is slightly soft it should be removed from the plant.

Bell Peppers

Benefits: Bell peppers are high in potassium, vitamins A, B6 and C and riboflavin.

Growing: Bell Pepper seeds should be sown indoors in a warm area and should be transplanted once the plant is approximately 20cm (8 inches) tall. Transplant into the soil and spread them about 61cm (2 feet) apart. Once the first fruit begins to appear lightly fertilise the soil. Support the plant with a bamboo stake.

Harvest: Bell peppers will mature in 60 to 90 days. As soon as the pepper is at a size similar to store bought brands you should remove it and store it in the fridge. Once harvested, bell peppers can last up to 10 days in storage.

Rhubarb

Benefits: Rhubarb is high in fibre, vitamins C, B and K, calcium, magnesium, potassium and manganese.

Growing: Before planting rhubarb be sure to remove all weeds from the soil. Plant rhubarb crowns in early spring in an area that gets bright sunlight for most of the day. Space rhubarb plants approximately 1.2 metres (4 feet) apart and 5cm (2 inches) deep and provide them with plenty of manure at the time of planting. Rhubarb requires plenty of water.

Harvest: You need to very patient with rhubarb as they need to grow for up to 3 years before they will begin to yield a viable crop. After this 3 year preparation period you should harvest the stalks once they are 38cm (15 inches) long. Do not remove all the stalks as the plant will die. Leave 2 or 3 stalks on the plant each growing season. Rhubarb plants can potentially live for up to 20 years.

Stews and soups

Stews and soups are a fantastic way to save money while getting somewhat nutritious food because they are cheap and easy to produce, can be made in bulk and can be frozen. Using the largest pot available, fill it with water and bring to the boil. Peel several potatoes and chop them up into rough cubes. Drop them into the pot along with any meat scraps available. Add a few chopped up carrots, some peas or whatever other vegetable that you have and allow this to cook for approximately 2 hours.

If you are in a position to buy a cut of meat, such as beef, it is important to cook this on a pan before adding to the stew. This will ensure that the meat is tender and provide rich beef flavouring to your stew.

Place the cubed beef on a hot pan and cook for several minutes, or until the outside of each cube is dark.

When freezing the remainder of your stew allow it to thoroughly cool to room temperature and try to fit it into several portion sized containers. When you need a meal simply defrost a single portion-sized container and heat it up in the microwave or a pot.

Always include some bread with your stew meal as this is great for mopping up the juices and sauce on the plate. It will also provide you with a bit more food. If you are able to make a large enough batch of stew it could easily last a week.

Soup packets, when used as a snack, can be fairly inexpensive, are quick to make, and provide a far healthier alternative to snacking on sweets. It is not a good idea to rely on these processed soups as your only source of food and should be combined with other meals, such as the stew you just made.

Urban farm animals

Keeping farm animals in your garden can be a very rewarding experience while providing you with food at the same time. If you decide to keep animals it is your responsibility to care for them properly. This will be a big step-up from growing food and will mean a lot more time being taken up catering for their needs. Farm animals should only be considered if you have the time it takes to care for and feed them properly.

The most popular urban farm animal and the only one I will discuss here are chickens. They should always be considered as pets and cared for just like the household cat or dog. Just like your dog, they require human company, attention and affection. Always ensure that they have plenty of food and water as well as adequate shelter from the elements.

A small, purpose built, chicken coup that is complete with a nestbox will be enough to house several chickens. Ensure that your back garden is well protected with walls or fences or your chickens may wonder off.

Chickens should be fed seeds and grains but can also eat some food scraps such as vegetables and fruit. These scraps should be cut into tiny pieces or pulsed in a blender to ensure they are small enough for the chicken to eat. If you have 4 chickens they can, in most cases, consume the food waste from a family of 6, thus negating the need to pay for organic waste disposal.

While chickens will consume just about anything, it is best if you avoid feeding them meat. Some of the more salty meats such as ham and bacon can cause the chicken to suffer from saline poisoning. Chickens that begin to suffer from saline poisoning will die very quickly. Chickens can also eat any chicken leftovers from dinner but that's just cannibalism, don't feed your chickens the remains of other chickens.

If kept in good health, chickens will provide you with approximately 1 egg per day. They have a tendency to take a day or two from laying eggs every 10 days or so. Keeping 4 chickens in your back garden can supply your family with a never-ending supply of free eggs. While purchasing eggs from the shop would seem to be far cheaper than keeping chickens in your back garden, it will work out cheaper for you, in the long run, to have your own supply from your mini urban farm. Chickens are generally quiet creatures with the cockerel being the loud alarm clock at ridiculous AM. If you do end up with a cockerel in your urban farm expect your neighbours to bombard you, the estate management, local council or local authority with a barrage of complaints. Just stick with the chickens.

Once each chicken outlives their usefulness and is no longer laying eggs feel free to have it for dinner. But wait... I said earlier that they should be considered the same as your pet cat or dog! That's right, and most people are incapable of slaughtering their chickens when the time comes. If you face this dilemma than it just means that you now have a retired chicken as a household pet. It will not be very expensive to allow this chicken to live out its life in your back garden, with the eggs produced throughout its lifetime being more valuable than its retirement upkeep. After all, this chicken will continue to consume food scraps that would ordinarily be thrown in the bin.

Potluck dinner bonanza

Being stuck in the poverty trap will greatly hinder your ability to enjoy nights out or socialise with friends. Going to an expensive restaurant will only leave you out-of-pocket and can dramatically increase your anxiety levels. To combat this you could host a potluck dinner night at your house once a month or once every two months. You really don't want to overdo this one, as it involves short-changing your friends, who will eventually figure out your scheme and you may lose them all.

In a potluck dinner, each guest brings a dish they prepare at home so that everyone can sample each other's food. The dish that you prepare for this event should, of course, be made as cheaply as possible. Your friends may bring far superior food and, the more friends invited, the more food available for you and your family.

Once the party is over, people will tend to leave their leftovers rather than taking them home to dump. This is your opportunity to gather a large amount of food and either freeze it or consume it over the next few days. Identify those foodstuffs that will go bad quickly and eat these first. Some things cannot be safely frozen, reheated and eaten, such as minced meat, so eat these dishes the next day.

You will need to reciprocate offers from your friends to attend their potluck events. This will be your chance to reward them for providing you with a lot of food. Prepare something slightly more expensive and tasty than you did before. Once the party is over, offer to help with the clean-up and subtly suggest that you could take the leftovers rather than dump them. This can be done in a way that does not draw too much suspicion from your friends, about your current financial situation, by complimenting the tasty dish you want to take home. Nobody will question your desire to bring one or two dishes home with you.

Farmers markets

Apart from providing you with healthy, organic, home or farm grown produce, farmers markets can be a treasure trove of free food. Most stalls will provide you with a free sample to sway you into purchasing their product. While some will openly advertise their free samples by presenting them, other stalls will require you to make enquiries about the product before being offered a taste. If you spend several hours going from stall-to-stall you may get enough free food to satisfy your hunger for a few hours or even for the rest of the day. Don't be timid when it comes to taking free samples, you are poor after all, but don't be too forward either. Clearing an entire plate or basket of free samples will draw the wrong kind of attention. Word will quickly spread around the market to be on the lookout for the greedy thief who is taking everything. You may quickly find that the free samples vanish from stalls until such time as you vanish from the market.

Become a known figure at the market by attending regularly and speaking with as many people as possible. Talk to the seller before buying something, even something small. If you can become known by this stall owner you will be favoured in the future with larger quantities for the same price and even the odd extra free item. When talking to the stall owner, be sure to ask them questions about what they do, how much work is involved, etc. The idea is to keep the stall owner talking as much as possible. Don't get too personal and don't ever tell them your current situation as it will just look like you are begging for food. They are intelligent enough to figure it out over time. Always give them compliments about the quality of their food and let them know that you would love to purchase more but can't afford it. Never look defeated and always maintain a bright outlook by smiling while talking to them. If you are lucky they will include extra items in your purchase, for free, or even give you something small without any purchase. Don't be pushy, have an enjoyable conversation and if you get anything extra consider it a bonus.

Most people neglect the very end of a farmers market. As they are begging to pack everything up for the day it may be a good idea to approach some sellers to see what kind of deals you can get. In some instances, perishable items will be dumped by the seller when they get home... why not offer to dispose of them? You may be lucky and get a large box of bananas or other perishable foods. Make the best of these perishable items before they go bad.

Importance of the shopping list

When your finances are in a particularly bad condition it is even more important to ensure that your grocery shopping list is 100% correct before entering the shop. By doing so you can help to eliminate unnecessary purchases which over time will drain your money faster than any other mistake.

Another vital component to grocery shopping is that you do not go when you feel hungry because you will find that unnecessary items with slowly but surely start creeping into your basket.

When writing the list, ensure that you only add items that are necessary for your survival such as meat, bread, dairy products, etc. All other items can be considered a luxury such as sweets or even coffee. Coffee can be very expensive and is simply not necessary for your survival. The only thing that you need to drink, right now, is water. Coffee and tea should be considered expensive luxury items.

When you are at the grocery store your mind should be focused only on the items in your list, everything else should be ignored. If you have made a mistake on the list do not get tempted to grab this item, just forget about it and you can get it next week. As the weeks go by you will become very adept at creating a perfect list. The reason for sticking so closely to the list is that once you start adding, even a single item, to your basket which is not on the list this behaviour can carry through in the following weeks and months.

When you get home, go through the receipts and write the price beside each item on your shopping list. This will allow you to calculate future grocery costs more carefully and also highlight the most expensive items. There may be something on the list that you can either do without or you may need to find a cheaper alternative.

By keeping track of the smallest detail you will be in a better position to budget your finances effectively. If you have a computer, this task can become easier and more effective by creating spreadsheets with vast amounts of data being stored and organised effectively.

Buying food in bulk

If you still have funds available it may be a good idea to start buying items in bulk. This is more than relevant to those items you tend to use all the time, that don't go bad, such as toiletries. Buying a full year's supply of toilet paper or shampoo may not seem like a good idea now but it will mean that each bottle of shampoo works out slightly cheaper. This system of bulk buying will work out as you become more strapped for cash. When doing the regular weekly shopping you will not need to include shampoo, toilet paper, or other such items. It will feel good to know that these items are sitting at home while you are struggling to pay for food.

Look around your home for items that are always used and make a list. Decide on how much you use and how often. For example, a bottle of shampoo might last 2 weeks or a month, so you would need to buy 26 bottles, or 12 bottles, depending on how much is used. The following list of items should be considered when buying in bulk:

- Toilet paper
- Shower gel
- Shampoo
- Conditioner
- Razor blades
- Sanitary products
- Cotton buds
- Batteries
- School and office supplies
- Laundry detergent
- Soap
- Trash bags
- Toothpaste
- Lightbulbs
- Tin foil (aluminium foil)
- Shrink wrap (saran wrap)
- Dishwasher detergent

Some food products can also be bought in bulk and should last for at least 1 year provided they are kept in suitable containers in the correct environment, such as:

- Butter
- Rice
- Pasta
- Nuts
- Cereal
- Dry pet food
- Dry beans
- Oatmeal

There is no real point in buying such large quantities of these items at face value so shop around for dedicated bulk buy stores or try to strike up a deal with the management to get the best price possible. Don't make excuses that there is no place to store them, create the space.

Free condiments

Every opportunity to receive free items should be taken advantage of as much as possible during times of financial distress. Many fast food outlets provide their customers with free condiments such as;

- Sause
- Salt
- Pepper
- Jams
- Sugar
- Salad dressings

These are usually small packets containing a small amount of each condiment. Take as many as you dare, but be warned that if you overdo it you may find yourself banned from this fast food outlet.

Gathering these items should be done over a long period of time rather than in a single day. Once you have a large enough collection of, let's say, a particular sauce, you could squeeze them into a larger bottle or container.

There is a large range of fast food restaurants offering free stuff with other types of businesses giving away free coffee, sugar packets, small containers of milk or even bread rolls. It is up to you to investigate and catalogue all those places within range of your home or along the routes that you regularly take in order to better plan a gathering journey. Keep a journal of what business, where it is and what they have to offer. If you are going to town for any reason, be sure to visit those places that are along your route and take a handful of free items, or whatever you think you can get away with taking. Be careful as some businesses absolutely require a purchase before you are allowed to take free condiments. If you just walk in and take them, without buying something, they could ban you from the store, or worse, have you arrested for theft.

Remember, now that you are poor it is time to effectively return to a hunter-gatherer instinct, taking advantage of unused or unwanted items wherever possible. This does not mean that you should become a hoarder, but rather someone who takes full advantage of free stuff.

The power of positive thinking

"Keep your face always toward the sunshine - and shadows will fall behind you."
Walt Whitman (1819-1892)

It is so easy, when faced with financial disaster, to only focus on the bad things that are happening to you, but this will actually draw to you, even more, reasons to feel negative. Positivity is not something that can be given to you; it is something you give to yourself. Only through a process of monitoring your thoughts can you identify the negative ones and take action to stop them.

Anytime a negative thought enters your mind, stop your thoughts immediately and think of them as a book. Each page will contain a single thought. Now just flip back a few pages to the negative one, rip out the page (in your mind), crumple it up in your hand and drop it on the ground. In real life, take your foot and squish the piece of paper into dust. This will seem very strange at the beginning, with your food stomping invisible things into the ground but it will have the effect of convincing your mind that you no longer want such thoughts. Now just think of something that makes you feel happy.

By remaining positive it will cause an immediate boost to your overall mood and outlook. This enhanced feeling of optimism will help you discover new and beneficial opportunities. Your mind will know that you don't want to just give up and are willing to do everything possible to secure your financial future.

There are always positive aspects to terrible situations, even going broke and facing crippling poverty, you just have to seek out the positive among all of that negative and focus intensely on it, so as to drown out the surrounding negative thoughts and feelings.

Gratitude

"If the only prayer you said in your whole life was, "thank you," that would suffice."
Meister Eckhart (1260-1328)

When you feel gratitude for the things you have in your life, no matter how small or seemingly insignificant, it has the effect of immediately boosting your mood. Once you begin being grateful for things you will suddenly find that the Universe will deliver more things to be grateful for. As this perpetual train of gratefulness continues you will find that life will begin to get better and better as the days go by.

Every morning, before getting up, spend at least 10 minutes on thinking of the things you are grateful for. This could be as simple as *"I am grateful for sleeping in this bed last night"* after all, things could always be worse, you could have woken up on the street. When you are finished thinking about things to be grateful for, write it down in a journal. By writing them down you can always refer to your list if things seem hard. Being grateful for things will also signal the brain to release Serotonin (the feel good drug) which will stay in your system for several hours. Only 10 minutes of gratitude in the morning can keep you happy for hours.

Another great way to express gratitude is to thank people who do something for you. If someone holds a door open for you give them a big heartfelt "*thank you*", especially if it is their job to hold the door open for you. If you are lucky enough to find some money on the ground, even if it is just a few cents, feel immense amounts of gratitude for this and in your mind say "***thank you, thank you, thank you***" and really feel the gratitude. If you're grateful for the small things, the Universe will line-up bigger and better things for you to be grateful for.

Any time you notice that your thoughts are drifting into the negative take that opportunity to instead search for things in your life to be grateful for. Close your eyes and think of just 3 things that cause you to feel gratitude. This can stop negativity in its tracks and make you feel happy and optimistic for a few hours.

Staying grounded

As crippling poverty takes hold and your life changes so dramatically, in such a short time, it is important to understand that everything happens for a reason... including your financial meltdown. Perhaps you were mismanaging your money to such an extent that the only way to learn your lesson was for the Universe to take it all away. Maybe you were destined to do something, such as a new career path or opening your own business but the only way to realise this was to destroy your way of life.

There are some things you can do, which will keep you grounded, while everything is crashing down around you.

- **Get in touch with nature.** Take this time in life to get yourself out and about. Go to wooded areas or other areas of spectacular natural beauty. If this is not possible then spend as much time as possible engaged in gardening or just sitting on a park bench. By doing so you will begin to realise that the stresses and anxiety will begin to slowly subside. While it won't go away it will be lulled gently into the background.

- **Sleep.** You need to get between 7-9 hours of good quality sleep every night. I know that financial pressure can keep you awake long into the night or even early morning so make time for sleep. If it is too difficult to get some shut-eye just go to bed earlier. Allow yourself to toss and turn for an hour or two but eventually, you will fall asleep.

- **Create habits.** Make sure that you get out of bed at the same time every morning, whether you are working or not and structure the remainder of the day around similar habits. This will help to keep you on the right track so that you don't fall into any bad or self-sabotaging behaviour.

When you are calm and grounded it will allow your mind to make better decisions and work efficiently towards those things you need to do. Remember that vast wealth can never make you happy, only you can make yourself happy. Stay focused on finding the happiness that already exists within you. Take frequent walks and enjoy the company of others. Stay grounded, stay strong, everything will be okay.

Taking intuitive action

By maintaining a positive outlook on life, the Universe will present opportunities. These could be in the form of potential job offers or an idea which may generate income and could grow into a flourishing business.

Most people are presented with such opportunities all the time but because they are not seeing them as signals from the Universe they never take the necessary action to realise whatever it is they are being presented with. Anytime an opportunity presents itself or when a strange series of coincidences are leading you somewhere, it is your job to take immediate action. You are being given an opportunity that must not be allowed to go unnoticed.

Every person you interact with could be a cog in the wheel of financial freedom for you so treat people as nicely as possible, you never know what could be offered at any time. If you can keep the image of a more financially successful future in your mind's eye than everything will conspire in your favour to bring this into fruition.

Always move forward and keep an ear out for anything that may be of benefit. It may seem like all the jobs in the world are taken and that you are now completely screwed but people get hired and fired every minute of every day. New business's open and new technologies come into existence all the time. Always strive forward towards your goal of financial freedom and eventually you can't help but get there. If you stop or move backwards you could be doomed. Never waste your evening by watching TV, instead try to learn something new. The more you learn, about everything and anything, the quicker you may come to seeing your future unfold in the way you want it to.

Expensive vices

"Men are more easily governed through their vices than through their virtues."
Napoleon Bonaparte (1769-1821)

It is perfectly normal to have something that saps our money. Maybe you collect DVD's or maintain a tropical marine aquarium. These expensive hobbies are fine while you are working and making money, but things like this can drain all of your savings in a very short time.

Taken to the extreme, you may have enjoyed full weekends of drinking, partying and snorting cocaine to the tune of hundreds of Euro. Now that you are faced with poverty it is time to identify and stop all such expensive vices. The only exception to this is if you smoke. While it would be very easy for me to preach about the dangers of smoking and the sheer expense involved, giving up the smokes is the last thing you should do right now. Things are bad and stress is, most likely, permeating every fibre of your being. Smoking, for a regular smoker, is necessary for keeping this stress at bay. It also has the added benefit of kerbing your hunger which can result in eating less food, thus saving some money. If you have never smoked, don't start now. Smokers should try to maintain their normal level of daily consumption with a view to slowly cutting down. Don't allow your financial stress to double the amount you smoke each day.

If you have any hobbies, write down what they are, how much they will cost you each month or each year. If any of your hobbies will result in expense within the coming year it is time for them to go. You can always take up this hobby once your finances have stabilised again. Gather up all the items related to your expensive hobby and sell all of it. The money is more important right now than holding onto a hobby that you will not be able to engage in.

If you enjoy a night of drinking on the weekends this will also need to stop... immediately. Instead, why not drive into town and have a soft drink or two. This way, you will get to enjoy a night out with friends without the massive expense and the debilitating hangover the following morning.

24-hour purchasing rule

Have you ever found yourself purchasing an item at the till, an item that you don't really want or need? This happens because manufacturers, advertisers and store owners have researched human behaviour to such an extent that they are able to trigger the purchasing mechanism in your brain using product placement, colours and text in certain formats which result in an impulse buy. These items are generally priced very low, which causes you to not even question the financial impact of such a purchase. It doesn't take too long for impulse purchases to add up every month.

It is important to formulate the habit of breaking this impulse buy system, instead always wait at least 24 hours before buying something you would not normally purchase. This 24-hour period will give you enough time to re-evaluate such a purchase, you could take this time to decide if you actually need the item or if it is good enough quality or if it's even within your budget and come up with an actual answer; should you buy this product or not.

The 24-hour rule should not only be applied to impulse buys or large purchases of, let's say, electronic goods but should also be applied to everything in your life including food. Do you really need to buy this fancy meal or could you make do with something cheaper?

I know how tempting it is to buy things on a whim but you are trying to combat crippling poverty, so remain strong willed and always question your purchasing decisions.

If you have engaged in any recent impulse buys it would be a good idea to look for the receipt today and return those items, if possible. Don't discount the value of this, potentially redeemable money, no matter how small an amount, because every penny counts right now.

When shopping for groceries, always check the upper and lower shelves, as more expensive items will be positioned at eye level to facilitate the store in maximising their profits. A lot of research has gone into the exact positioning of products, even food, in order to manipulate human behaviour.

Lasting purchases

Now that you are poor, it is time to rethink the items you purchase and how you care for them. In the past, when you had money it would have seemed perfectly acceptable to buy a new piece of clothing when something small, and easily fixable, happened like a button falling off, or a small rip. I'm pretty sure that when you got some takeaway food that far too much of it was dumped when you were finished. Wasting food or dumping clothing is no longer an option.

When you buy clothes, be sure that they are good quality, with tight stitching and don't have any loose threads hanging off. There is a misconception in society that the more expensive an item is the better quality and longer lasting it is. With most items, the exact opposite is the case. The reason for this is because, if you could afford to buy the expensive item in the first place, you can buy it again in a year or so when it fails.

Apart from checking the quality of clothes before purchasing them, it is important to learn how to stitch and make repairs, in order to make them last as long as possible. There are countless tutorial videos on the internet which describe how to sew on a button or repair a rip. Some videos even show how to turn one or more unwanted garments into a new piece of clothing. Spend some time researching these tutorials and bookmark the most useful of these. Start with something small like sewing on a button. If you have never repaired clothing before it is a good idea to get a large, sealable container for storing seamstress supplies such as;

- Needles
- Pins
- Pincushion
- Thread
- Scissors
- Rotary cutter
- Cutting mat
- Seam ripper
- Spare buttons
- Ribbons
- Measuring tape
- Safety pins

Repairing clothes is not just for the ladies, men are more than capable of repairing their own clothes or sewing on their own buttons. Nearly every army in the world teaches new recruits how to sew and make repairs to their clothing.

When buying food it is important to remain vigilant of sell-by-dates and the general condition of perishable items such as fruit. To save on food waste, consume those items that will go bad first before anything else. Keep a prioritised list on your fridge or other convenient location that will quickly show you what food needs to be cooked and eaten first. This will save a lot on general food waste which will ultimately save you money in the long run.

Pets

"Dogs are our link to paradise. They don't know evil or jealousy or discontent. To sit with a dog on a hillside on a glorious afternoon is to be back in Eden, where doing nothing was not boring--it was peace."
Milan Kundera (1929-)

I know that beloved fur ball is pretty much one of the family now, but they will also need to cut back on luxuries just like you. One of the first things to do is change their cans of food to a far cheaper version. This will become problematic as your cat or dog will have become accustomed to getting the good, name brand food so it is best if you replace every 3rd can with the cheaper alternative. Do this for the first week before making every 2nd can be one of the expensive ones. Over a period of 1 month, slowly switching from named brand pet food to the cheaper alternative can bring your pet to the point where they become accustomed to this cheaper version. Don't get me wrong here, your pet will know it's getting the inferior product so expect him or her to throw you dirty looks for the foreseeable future.

If you previously pampered your pet with needless accessories or pedicures it is time to stop this immediately. You don't need to wean your dog from a weekly pedicure as the animal never wanted any of this in the first place, this was all just for you. The only exception to this rule is if you have a dog with thick fur which needs to be trimmed during the hot summer months. This trimming should be done at the beginning of the summer and limited to once per year.

Many animals can survive perfectly well on food scraps that we would normally throw away. After each meal, gather anything that your pet may eat in a container and use this as their evening meal. This will slightly reduce the amount of tinned food used for feeding your pet which can produce slight savings over time.

If your finances are in such a terrifying state that you are no longer able to feed your pet regularly or find yourself unable to afford a yearly visit to the vet you must consider the possibility of giving your pet away to a family who can provide such care. I know this one will be very hard to bear but it will be far better for the animal in the long run.

Special occasions and gift giving

"Books make great gifts because they have whole worlds inside of them. And it's much cheaper to buy somebody a book than it is to buy them the whole world!"
Neil Gaiman (1960-)

The sheer expense involved with Christmas, birthdays, christenings or other large events can, and will, cause some of the highest levels of anxiety and stress imaginable to those whose finances are in dire straights. If you were previously in a position where you showered everyone with gifts it is time to change this dramatically. You can no longer afford to spend thousands of Euros per year on gifts for everyone and anyone.

Take action as soon as your financial situation comes under threat by talking to your family. Explain that, from now on you will only be able to get small gifts for everyone at Christmas time and no other gifts through the year. This means that they will not be getting birthday presents from you or for any other occasion. Impose a spending limit, maybe €10 per person. If you need to get gifts for 5 people at Christmas time you know that your budget for an entire years' worth of gift giving is only going to be €50. This will immediately alleviate most of the stress involved with gift giving.

Don't get greedy and make sure that the same spending limit applies to the gifts they will be getting you. It is best if you can give them suggestions of items that you really need. While Christmas is supposed to be a time for receiving items you like or want it is now time to get very practical. Maybe you need a new toaster or kettle. Christmas is your chance to replace broken items around your home.

If you can't think of any items that are needed around the home you could suggest that they get you consumable goods such as toilet paper, shampoo or dishwasher detergent. I know, sounds terrible, but you are no longer in a position to enjoy frivolous gifts. Once your financial situation has changed for the better you can enjoy

Christmas gifts properly but for now, use this opportunity to get things you need.

Is it common for people in your workplace to get gifts for each other at every possible opportunity? This needs to end, right now. You may be isolating yourself to your work colleagues but all you can do is explain that times are hard at the moment.

Homemade crafts

There is a way to give gifts on other occasions besides Christmas, by creating your own craft items at home. As long as it can be done with zero expense, using various materials that are either lying around your home or scavenged, then you will still be able to stay within your €50 gift giving budget but also join in the celebrations and giving involved in birthdays and other special occasions.

There are plenty of instructional videos available on the internet and don't worry if you have never made gifts before or think that you cannot do it, with a little practice it will be possible to create stunning and original craft items in no time.

When shopping in second-hand stores and charity shops, be on the lookout for craft items such as:

- Crayons
- Coloured pencils
- Paints
- Textures & yarn
- Toothpicks
- Clay
- Straws
- String
- Beads
- Buttons
- Fishing line
- Ink pads
- Glitter
- Glue sticks
- Scissors
- Coloured tissue paper
- Cans & jars
- Styrofoam & bubble wrap
- Empty boxes

If you can build up a supply of craft items cheaply, or for free, they will always be on-hand which will negate the need for panic buying as an event approaches. Depending on what you are crafting there can be a wealth of supplies in your back garden or neighbourhood, such as:

- Dried leaves
- Sticks
- Flowers
- Pine cones
- Feathers
- Small rocks or stones

This will be a time for great creativity on your part but such activities will also help to ease the stress associated with crippling poverty and provide you with a great sense of pride and accomplishment.

In our current consumer culture, these handmade crafts can be appreciated more than something you buy at the store. People will tend to appreciate the effort involved and the personalised approach to such a gift, with many of these creations taken pride-of-place in the home of the receiver.

Special occasions do not need to cost a small fortune and can be easily enjoyed, even if you are completely broke.

Making extra money

"The longer you're not taking action the more money you're losing."
                                        Carrie Wilkerson

Regardless of whether you now find yourself unemployed, or if the income from your full-time job just doesn't cover the costs of living, it is important to make as much extra cash as possible. This is especially true if you are also facing mounting debts and struggle to make your repayments.

Cash jobs are by far the best option because you don't need to declare these for tax purposes, but bear in mind that **you are supposed to**. By not declaring this extra income you will be breaking the law so be sure to weigh up your options and question your own moral compass about tax evasion.

There are a lot of jobs that people just don't want to do and will gladly pay someone to alleviate them of this burden. Become very inventive when looking for such household tasks or menial labour jobs that nobody else wants to do. There are a lot of opportunities available in your local neighbourhood or city. Who knows, one of these opportunities could grow into a flourishing business venture.

Cutting lawns

There is only one successful way to generate money from cutting other people's lawns and that's to approach as many houses as possible, as fast as possible. Expect that for every 100 houses approached, only 1 of these will accept your proposal to work on their lawn. If you charge €10 per job it can turn into an extremely long day for such little return.

In saying that, €10 per day over 7 days (€70) can put enough food on the table, or pay for heating. If you are unemployed, do not discount this money making resource. The numbers above may change dramatically because you will not be some kid trying to earn extra pocket money. This will go one of two ways, you will either be looked upon as someone who is really trying and attract more work or you will not be welcomed at all.

Always bring a rake and a roll of empty garbage bags. Ensure that the deal involves leaving the grass cuttings at the customer's house as you can't be expected to drag these bags with you all day. Be sure to do the most professional job possible as this could mean repeat business.

When it comes to cutting other people's lawns for extra cash you just have to go for it.

Washing cars

There are very few people who genuinely enjoy the weekly chore of washing their car. Most people just view this task as yet another housework thing that they need to get over and done with as fast as possible with many choosing to pay for this to be done at a petrol station or dedicated car wash facility. Why not do it for them and make some money while you're at it.

There is no way that you will get away with charging a lot for this, as the petrol station may charge between €5-€10 so try to keep your charge within this range. You will need to bring all the cleaning equipment with you, such as:

- Large bucket
- Sponges
- Squeegee
- Microfiber towels
- Chamois leather shammy
- Detergent

Just like a window washer you can carry all of the equipment in the large bucket with the homeowner supplying water. This task will be 1 to 2 hours of hard work for a very small return but if you can establish regular customers and do a thorough and professional job it can result in tips and extras from your customers.

This could be turned into a weekend job with up to 10 customers spread out over Saturday and Sunday that could potentially bring in €50-€100.

Dog walker

If you have a dog then you know that it must be walked on a daily basis, without exceptions. Can you remember what this was like when you were in full-time employment? It may have been a struggle for you to do this daily task while still juggling everything else that needed to be done. Believe it or not, other people are far busier than you were on those work days and would love to have a dog walking service to alleviate some of the pressure they are under.

While dog walkers are popular in America there is no reason that you cannot start the trend where you live. You will need to generate some customers, either by going door-to-door offering your services or by approaching people who are currently walking their dog.

A reasonable charge would be between €5 and €10 for 1 hour, with a small group of, let's say 6 dogs bringing in between €30 and €60 per day. You will need to arrange that all dogs are available at the same time each day so that you can collect them, walk them and return them in the shortest time possible. Some people will try to take advantage by getting you to mind their dog all day. Don't allow this to happen even once, and charge a full day's walking service if you are left minding their pet all day.

When dog walking, bring a large stick to help defend the pack and begin investing in your own, very secure leads, as you may not be able to rely on the one provided by the owner. It may be flimsy or break.

There is a market out there for dog walkers; you just need to find customers.

Recycle for cash

In some countries or regions, a recycling system may operate, where plastic bottles or metal tins can be traded for cash. Depending on where you live this may be done through local shops or at dedicated centres. While the amount of money paid per item will be very small it is worth keeping an eye out for such items discarded on the street or in trash cans. Every time you see one, bring it home and clean it. Store these in your shed or outhouse until you have a large enough collection to warrant a trip to your local centre.

Do not dump these items in your back garden or you will quickly get yourself into trouble with the local council, regional government, environmental protection agency or whatever organisation deals with the dumping of garbage in your local area. Ensure that these items are properly cleaned and stored correctly. Plastic bottles should be kept separate from tin cans, etc. Never store these items in the trunk of your car as you may need to sell this car in a hurry, to make ends meet or your vehicle may be facing repossession and you will lose these recycling items as a result.

Even a large amount of these items may only bring in an extra €5 or €10 per month but when you are chronically poor these small amounts of money could make all the difference.

Stay out of trouble

This one should go without saying, but staying out of trouble will get more and more difficult for you, especially as bills and demands come in the letterbox in ever increasing frequency. There are plenty of unsavoury characters that will try to take advantage of your vulnerable situation to convince you to do jobs which are highly illegal. Don't deal drugs, perform burglaries or rip people off.

Let's say that you decide to deal drugs temporarily so that you can get a bit of the pressure off. That's a great idea; drugs pretty much sell themselves and can be highly profitable. The only problem is that you are broke, so where will you get the money to buy your first consignment of drugs? That's not a big problem for drug suppliers as they will freely give them to you so you can begin dealing. It's at this stage that all of your problems begin, and they won't go away very easily. As the drugs will be considered a loan you will be charged interest, to such a large extent that you may never be able to properly pay back this debt. As a result, the drug suppliers will continue to use you as a dealer long after the first consignment has been sold. You will find yourself working highly unsocial hours, in constant danger, for very little pay. In effect, you will turn into an employee of the drug supplier.

Maybe you already have enough money to purchase a large consignment of drugs so do not need to take the dangerous route of getting drugs on loan. Great... now all you have to do is sell it all and sit back in your giant mansion sipping cocktails. The problem with this is, you will not make so much money to retire on and it will be very difficult and dangerous to sell those drugs in the first place. When you were an employee of the drug supplier you were under their protection from other drug dealers, but now that you are on your own, that protection is gone. If another dealer finds you selling drugs on his patch you face the ever-present risk of being killed. Also, if you are caught by the police expect to receive a harsh jail sentence.

Do yourself a favour and remain vigilant for trouble so that you can stay as far away from it as possible, no matter how tempting it may be.

Grab hold of opportunities

Now that you are poor it is vital to seize any opportunity to make some money. Be careful not to jump into anything that can get you into trouble, with the law or other people, yet at the same time don't think over an opportunity for too long or someone else might take it.

Now is the time to become even more outgoing and sociable than ever. This doesn't mean that you should be going to the pub every night or attending an expensive get-together, it just means that you should talk to everyone and anyone. There are plenty of people out there with money to spend on varying different dilemmas they face but can't seem to figure out how to get someone to help them. Perhaps they need the badly overgrown back garden to be cleared, but can't find a handyman to take care of the job. Everyone they approach may be professionals who are charging extortionate rates.

If someone begins to tell you such a story it is your chance to enquire how much they are willing to spend on the job, and then offer to view the area which needs to be cleared. Who knows, the work and pay may be reasonable to you. It is important, when carrying out such work, that you do the best you can and always clean up properly after yourself. If you do a good job there could be further work down the line due to word-of-mouth.

Once you open yourself up to receiving such opportunities they will seem to come out of nowhere on a constant basis. What you don't know is that these opportunities were always there, but because you already had money they were completely ignored by your subconscious mind.

It doesn't need to be odd handyman jobs either. If you speak with enough people you may discover a job opportunity or change in career that you may not have otherwise considered.

Cashing in

"If stock market experts were so expert, they would be buying stock, not selling advice."
Norman Ralph Augustine (1935-)

Throughout our life, it is normal to make investments, in stock, property or other business ventures. If you are fortunate to have any such investments it is time to cash it all in. If you hold any stock, sell it today, even if it means taking a loss because you need cash right now. Some savings incentives, or bonds, may take 10+ years to mature properly and, while cashing them in may incur a massive loss from your initial investment, you can always begin such a bond again when your financial situation has improved.

While the property market worldwide has taken a big hit since the economic crash of 2008 it may be necessary to sell any properties you own, which are not your main home. This includes any rental properties or summer houses. The only exception to this is if you have rental properties, which contain tenants and provides a steady monthly income. If this is the case then you are not as poor as you may think, with a few changes in spending habits being the solution to your implied poverty.

I know these things may be a long-term investment for your retirement, but you may be years from retiring while your finances dictate that you need money today.

Selling your personal possessions will be a real eye-opener, as almost everything you own is now only worth a small fraction of what it originally cost to purchase. Let's say you decide to sell your 3-year-old laptop, which you bought for €1,000. Laptops with a similar specification to yours are currently selling, brand new, for maybe €500. Unfortunately, nobody wants it, they would prefer to spend €500 on a new one, so when you do eventually sell it, it might only fetch €150-€200. That's a big loss and you will be left feeling cheated and hard-done when everything is finally sold. It will seem like you are sitting on a gold mine of stuff but this is not true. This should not discourage you from selling your things. If your finances are that bad then, by all means, sell it all. Perform enough research before selling an item to be sure you are not charging below the current asking price, especially when it comes to antique items.

Downgrading

From the moment you realise that poverty will take hold you must think about immediately downgrading everything in your life. This includes your house, car, TV subscription, consumption of resources and anything else you can think of.

If you have a car, gather all the documentation and bills from the past year. Add up the cost of insurance, road tax, repairs, fuel and yearly servicing. This is potentially the amount of money needed to run this vehicle for the upcoming year. Do you have that kind of money available to you right now?

If you don't have the money to keep your car then you will need to downgrade, however, this should be a radical change. It will be almost the same cost per year if you trade in your 5.0-litre twin turbo to a 4.8-litre version. Let's stay with the example of a gigantic, fuel guzzling 5.0-litre vehicle. This might cost you €5,000 per year to operate (at a very conservative estimate), but a 1.0-litre basic car might only cost you €2,900 per year. If you made such a downgrade today it would result in immediate savings of €2,100 per year.

Yes, I know that you really want that cool 5.0-litre car; after all, you spent years getting to a position where your dream car was finally realised. Unfortunately for you, that dream has come crashing down and you must accept the reality of your financial situation.

The same goes for your house. If you own a house it would probably be a good idea to sell it and buy a much smaller place. The difference could end all of your financial problems within a month or two, depending on how radical this downgrade is. All of your debts could be accounted for, but just like the car, it is something that you will need to accept before action can be taken.

It may be tempting to sell the house and buy a small apartment but these have yearly maintenance charges attached, which could by up to €2,000. Owning your own house is a cheaper option in the long run. Don't get tempted to downgrade to such an extent that you sell your home in favour of renting an apartment because the cost of renting is always higher than a long-term mortgage.

A similar approach should be taken for every major possession. If you have been fortunate enough to own an aeroplane, boat or any other large extravagance, sell it now. This should clear your debts and provide you with several years' worth of survival money, thus negating the need to downgrade other areas of your life.

Do you really need those

Over the years you have probably bought tonnes of stuff, furniture, ornaments, jewellery, watches, electronics, entertainment items and even things related to hobbies. If your finances are in complete meltdown it might be time to sell all of your possessions. Now, you may be thinking that you are sitting on a gold mine of stuff, but these things will not be worth, even close to, what you think they are worth.

Take a full day to walk around your home and list all the items that you are willing to part with. Just list the item in a journal and leave it where it is for now. Beside each item draw 3 distinct columns and title them:

- Original cost
- Expected sale price
- Actual sale price

Fill in the sections *"original price"* and *"expected sale price"*. If you can no longer remember what you paid for the item give your best estimate. In the column *"expected sale price"* come up with a realistic sounding estimate of what you think the item is worth to sell second-hand. Using the internet, find local sales channels that apply to your country, region, county or city and search for those items to see what other people are selling them for. Once you begin to see that items are selling for a lot less than you thought, and you have sufficiently recovered from the shock of this realisation, there is a little bit more bad news, they will not sell for the price listed. It is safe to say that the average price for your item or similar items will actually sell for about 60% of that value.

As you can see, your beloved possessions are worth far less than first thought. You can use these selling websites to list your own items but research these carefully to determine any charges that may apply. Some sites will want an upfront charge (these should be avoided); while others will want a small charge once the sale is complete. When selling second-hand items come up with 2 figures, the price you will list the item for and the absolute minimum you are willing to accept. People will always try to undercut your price but if you have an absolute minimum value set this will dictate your selling pattern. **Never sell below this minimum value**.

Take enough time to list the item correctly by taking good quality pictures and attempt to answer any questions you may be asked in the description. This will help to eliminate unnecessary work later, as those questions are already answered for the prospective buyer.

Second-hand stores

"Let us not be too particular; it is better to have old second-hand diamonds than none at all."
Mark Twain (1835-1910)

The vast majority of people, who have been financially stable for a long time, may have never ventured into a second-hand clothes store or charity shop but if you are reading this book it is time to change this behaviour. Second-hand stores and charity shops offer some unbeatable bargains with most of the items being in an acceptable condition for use. There are sometimes designer clothing or other high-end items being sold at rock-bottom prices.

Utilise this valuable money-saving resource for your yearly clothes shopping. When you first begin visiting these stores check as many as possible to see what they have to offer. After a while, some will become places you visit regularly. Those stores you frequent the most could give you a lot of little extras if you take the time to strike up conversations with the staff. Over time, as they get to know you, they may hold onto really good quality items so you can have the first refusal or may include some small extras every time you make a purchase.

As an example, a designer jacket that may cost €500 new could sell in these charity shops for as little as €5-€10. Almost all charity and second-hand stores will provide clothing that has been washed and pressed. This jacket, being a designer labelled item, may have been very well cared for by its previous owner.

Depending on where you live, these shops could provide a wide range of items such as:

- Clothes
- Shoes
- Books
- Jewellery
- Household items
- Furniture
- Pet care supplies
- Electronic equipment
- Or any number of other items

While all the items in charity shops will have been donated, the staff may be able to point you in the right direction when it comes to selling your own personal items. Apart from charity shops, there could also be thrift shops (euro shops), that can provide common household items and food for far cheaper than the large chain stores, however, not all items are cheaper so do some research before making any purchases.

Always dress well

It is very easy, when you become poor, to dress poorly. Let's face it... what reason do you have to dress like a million dollars? You don't have a million dollars, you don't have anything, and you're poor, hungry, what's the point in anyth..... STOP! Do you see how a simple thing like how you decide to dress in the morning can, and will, allow negative thoughts and feelings to creep in?

When you dress like a million bucks you will feel like a million bucks. Take the example of meeting with and speaking to, someone who may be in a position to offer you a job or knows someone that they can recommend you to. Let's look at this scenario from two points:

1. You are dressed in sweat pant, t-shirt and running shoes. When you meet this person they will form an initial impression of you, starting with your shoes and working their way up. What they will see is someone who doesn't really care that much about their appearance. If you don't care about yourself that much, how will you possibly care about any job that could be offered?

2. You are dressed in stylish shoes, slacks and a matching shirt. Your leather belt appears to be good quality and the colours all seem to match well. You will be immediately judged as a person of high moral standards with attention to detail. Because you are dressed well and know it, this will shine through in your vibrant smile and energy. The job is most likely yours before you even speak.

Everywhere you go there are people who have the potential to help you. If their impression of you is a negative one that help will never arrive. If however, they see someone who will always take pride in themselves, opportunities and assistance will flow your way.

Dumpster diving

This is probably not the best or most hygienic of activities. It may not even pay off. When dumpster diving, bear in mind that you may need to search through countless dirty skips before you discover anything of value.

Warning: Do not scavenge for food in dumpsters or bins, weather sealed in a package or not, as this food will most likely make you violently ill. It's not worth the risk.

In some countries, dumpster diving or retrieving items from bins is illegal and will carry penalties if caught. In May 2015 a couple were arrested in Sunderland, UK when they were discovered taking food from the back of a large grocery store. This food was out-of-date and destined for the dump. The large containers of food were waiting outside the back of the building before they would be loaded on bin trucks. Thankfully, in this case, the judge was very lenient considering the couple were poverty stricken. It shows that even food that is being thrown away can get you arrested if you steal it.

Before dumpster diving, ensure that you are familiar with the laws in your region. Get your mind prepared as you may encounter some of the most disgusting things imaginable while sifting through discarded waste. You will not be very productive, in this endeavour, if you spend all of your time retching and dry heaving. Always wear appropriate clothing while dumpster diving. Use your household work clothes or even better set aside specific clothing for this task and make sure you have protective gloves and a bright headlamp.

Even if it is perfectly legal for you to take items from dumpsters and bins it will be heavily frowned upon by store managers, householders with a skip outside their door, and the general public so be as sneaky as possible. Thoroughly clean any items you scavenge and shower very well after a dumpster diving trip.

Coupons

Depending on where you live, coupons for local shops, large chain stores or online purchases can provide massive savings if combined correctly. While it is very common to find such cost-cutting coupons in America it may not be an option if you live in Europe.

Newspapers and magazines often provide coupons on a monthly or weekly basis, either loosely or as part of the printed material. Always check discarded newspapers and magazines for unused or unwanted coupons, cut them out and file them away at home until you can figure out the best combination that provides the maximum savings.

In some instances, they may only produce huge savings if you purchase items in ridiculously large quantities, such as 100 bottles of shampoo for €10 but this should never discourage you. Think about it, 100 bottles of shampoo will last you and your family for a very long time. Having such large quantities will also mean that you don't have to worry about buying it in the future, thus putting a little less strain on your weekly shopping trips.

Become friendly with your local newsagent as they usually dump massive amounts of newspapers and magazines every evening or at the end of each week. These could turn out to be a gold mine of savings due to the hundreds of coupons that can be gathered. The only problem you will now face is dumping all of these newspapers.

Be warned that using coupons will lead to purchasing things you would not normally buy. If this happens too often it may lead to that product being added to your weekly grocery shopping. While it worked out financially when you were using the coupons, buying such an item at the regular price could be a lot more expensive than an alternative product.

Store cards (not credit cards) can offer savings also by their use of points. Every time you buy an item it is worth a certain amount of points which can either be redeemed on future purchases or may be provided as money-off coupons once per month. Check each store's points policy carefully and apply for as many as you can. The only problem with the shops who refund the points as monthly coupons is that they will be for the named brand version of products you may already be buying the cheaper alternative of. They are trying to get you to switch to the more expensive version in order to maximise their profits, don't fall for this one.

Utility bills

"Electricity is really just organized lightning."
George Carlin (1937-2008)

When you were working and earning money there was probably never any thought to putting on the heating in the house or leaving your computer or TV turned on all day. Now that you are poor these activities can drain your savings very quickly. Even if you have savings it is important to take immediate action to kerb your utility expenses.

Ensure that the lights are turned off when you are leaving any room for more than 15 minutes. If you are moving from room-to-room repeatedly, it will actually cost more money to turn the lights on and off all the time. If you know that the room will be empty for more than 15 minutes turn the lights off. When a light bulb is turned on, it will rely on a burst of electricity to start a reaction of heating the filament before settling down to using a trickle of power.

This initial surge can add up if the light is repeatedly turned on and off.

Become economical when using large electrical items such as the washing machine. Only do a load of washing when you can fill the machine. It is a huge waste of resources, and money, to only wash a few garments at a time. Always monitor the weather conditions and hang your clothes out to dry wherever possible, as the dryer can cost a lot to run.

Vampire eyes can also cost a lot over time. *"Vampire eyes"* is the term given to the tiny red lights from electronic equipment that is left on standby. Ensure that all TV's, DVD players, satellite decoder boxes, etc. are fully switched off and plugged out after each use. Just because your satellite system may or may not record a single 30-minute show during the evening is absolutely no excuse to leave it plugged in all night. You are too poor to allow such a frivolous thing to cost you more money.

When you leave electrical and electronic items plugged in, even if they are fully turned off and not on standby, there is still a tiny electrical charge travelling through the power cable. This is costing you money, all the time. Plug out everything that is not being used. The only exception to this rule is if the plug sockets have individual activation switches. If you can turn the power off from the plug socket itself, then get into the habit of always doing this. All of these tiny electricity surges will add up over time.

If you pay for domestic water supply, make sure the dishwasher is full before turning it on. Do not think that water can be saved by using the kitchen sink for cleaning the dishes. The dishwasher will be far more efficient when it comes to water consumption. Using the sink should only be considered if you live alone and don't use enough cutlery and kitchenware to fill a dishwasher. Never turn on the dishwasher before it is absolutely full, as this can add up to significant unnecessary charges over the long term.

Cheaper electricity

Electricity is by far the most consumed resource of any household and should be the first one to reduce when facing crippling poverty. Depending on where you live and which electricity supplier you are with, they may have a cheaper tariff during certain periods of the day. The time of day would depend entirely on the company themselves and may be during anti-social hours, such as after midnight.

Take some time to study the contract you have with your electricity supplier, what they charge and when. If your supplier does provide cheap electricity during certain hours it is best if you schedule large-scale electricity use around this time. Let's say that your electricity will be cheaper after midnight, you should use the washing machine and dryer after this time. In the long-run, the savings from this cheaper tariff will begin to pay off. The biggest drawback with doing this is the effect of noise on you, your family and potentially your neighbours. Given enough complaints from your neighbours, you could end up in trouble, especially if you live in a gated community or housing estate with strict management regulations.

It may also be a good idea to research all of the suppliers in your region as there are many deals available for switching accounts. These deals will usually last for the first 6 months, however switching again after 6 months can continue the cycle of savings. Most people stay with their current supplier forever because it is easier but this can exclude you from the possibility of making some big savings when it comes to your utility bills.

When switching accounts, some of the important questions to ask are;

- *"Do I have to sign-up for a contract that goes beyond this 6 months introductory deal?"*
- *"What times of day provide the cheapest rates?"*
- *"Is there a penalty for switching suppliers at the end of the introductory period?"*
- *"Are there any hidden charges?"*

Depending on your current financial situation it may be worth outfitting your home with renewable energy harvesting systems such as solar panels or wind turbines. This, of course, would only apply to those who have vast savings and can long foresee financial disaster in the coming months as these technologies can cost huge sums of money in order to be cost effective. If you are in a position to have solar panels installed they have the potential, combined with passive house technologies to actually generate income for your household. Some people are paid annually by their electricity supplier for the extra power they generate at home.

If you are lucky enough to have a fast flowing stream running through your property than a micro hydro electrical generator may be capable of providing all of your household needs. These generators typically cost €1,000 (USD$1,094), are easy to install and require little to no maintenance. Depending on the flow rate of the river or stream that is flowing through your property, micro hydro electrical generators can prove to be the least expensive option when generating your own electricity and should be the first thing you consider, but only if you have a river or stream on your property.

Banking

"The modern banking system manufactures money out of nothing."
Josiah Stamp (1880-1941)

When you become poor it will get increasingly expensive to maintain a bank account and the services they provide. Should your funds dry up it is still possible to continue drawing out money in the form of an overdraft. This is essentially a short-term, high-interest loan from the bank that typically must be repaid within 1 week and can carry an interest rate of up to 5,000%. Banks are notorious for having a severe lack of transparency when it comes to fees and charges, which quickly become far more transparent only after you have incurred huge fees.

Being poor will mean that you are constantly living on the edge, with very exact amounts of money coming and going from your account that only covers the exact cost of goods and services. It will be very easy to stray into the negative on your account.

When this happens fees will be immediately applied and because of this marginal living method, such fees will take forever to fully pay off, while incurring more fees until it's cleared.

Depending on where you live and the kind of bank account held you may be charged a fee every time you use an ATM. These small charges will quickly mount up. In order to mitigate these charges, it is best if you either withdraw money from the bank in person or withdraw the maximum possible when using an ATM.

The average cost, per person, per year in bank charges is €150. This money could cover basic food needs for a few weeks or cover special occasions like Christmas. If at all possible, abandon your bank account in favour of cash only transactions, checking services or a local credit union.

Stop investing in banks

Banks, by their nature, are designed to allow for defaulters. This could include people who do not pay their credit card bills or fail to meet their mortgage payments. They genuinely don't care if you fail because it is all built into the system. Unfortunately, this also means that they don't care about you, or your financial situation when you do fail. During the process of your savings slowly dwindling away to nothing, the banks will impose hefty charges and late fees, which will inevitably quicken the pace of your ultimate default.

The best option, if possible, is to move your money to a local credit union or investment cooperative. The advantage of being a member of the credit union is that they don't want people to default. They will work with you at a far more reasonable level than a bank. Most credit union accounts offer higher interest rates on savings and slightly lower interest rates on loans.

The biggest disadvantage of credit unions is that many do not have ATM facilities, electronic transfer between companies and other banks, online banking or credit card facilities.

It is extremely difficult these days, to completely abandon a regular bank in favour of a local credit union but if you could just move your savings from the bank it will, over time, deliver bigger interest payments than you could have received from the bank.

Local credit unions are a little bit more lenient when it comes to offering loans. If you have recently lost your job and the bank will not issue a small short-term loan, a credit union may be in a position to give it to you, however, you will need to have already established a relationship with the credit union first. Open an account with them as soon as possible. Don't wait until you are starving and practically homeless. You may have up to 1 year before the worst happens so act now.

Stop all automatic debits

Banks make things very convenient by providing the ability to pay for utility bills and other ongoing expenses with automatic debits. This facility is great as it provides you with the convenience to perform banking duties without taking time off work to deal with companies in person but these automated systems will become a real big problem when your account finally runs dry. For each missed payment, the bank will impose charges, plus the company being paid may impose interest payments on top of your original bill.

Attempt to stop all automated debits from your bank and deal with utility companies themselves. It may be possible to pay your bills in one of their offices directly. This will ensure that you pay by cash or cheque only, which will have the added effect of making you far more conscious of usage. It is very easy to neglect the upcoming costs of electricity usage if it just seems to magically get paid every month. When you have to part with your hard earned cash in person you will instinctively begin to use far less electricity. The same principle goes for all other utilities and payments that you are currently making on a monthly basis.

It will become difficult to pull this off if you are still in full-time employment but some utility companies are open on Saturdays to facilitate in-person payments. You will need to contact all of your utility companies to find out if it is possible to pay your bills in person, by post or through wire transfer.

Once all automated debits are successfully stopped it will also mean that you don't need to deal with the bank as often but also if these payments were the last service a bank was providing you with, it is safe to finally close your account and deal with local credit unions instead.

Pay-day loans

Pay-day loans are provided by private lending companies to people who would ordinarily be turned down by the bank or are unable to secure a credit card for themselves. As a result, the pay-day loan company will charge unbelievable interest rates on these short-term loans. They are specifically designed for people with a job because payment will be made very quickly. Unfortunately for you, they will also loan money to people without a job, and they love doing this because when the loan is not paid back on time the gigantic interest rates kick into high gear.

These short-term lending companies have existed in certain countries for decades, with their regulation being dramatically relaxed in those countries that never had them before, following the worldwide economic crash of 2008. Some of these companies can charge over 10,000% interest per annum with the average, depending on where you live, at around 3,500% APR.

The main attraction with such loans is that they are generally provided without requiring a credit check or proof of employment. While it may seem to be a severe disadvantage for a lending company to give out such risky loans, which may not be paid back, it is those people who do not pay back the loan that actually drives the industry forward. If you do not pay them on time, massive interest will begin to pile up and they will pursue and hound you incessantly for payment.

If you do default on one of these loans you will face the problem of dealing with very aggressive debt collectors who may have the power to automatically withdraw money from your bank account. They will certainly harass you for payment at your home and place of work. One of the worst case scenarios when dealing with debt collectors is they have the power to repossess everything you own. If the items taken from you do not meet the total owed, they will continue to pursue you for the balance.

These pay-day lenders will repeatedly encourage you to take out more and more loans, even if you are making the correct payments, in an effort to trap you in an endless cycle of debt and charges.

Payday lenders should be avoided at all costs. It would be better to starve than engage with them.

Credit cards

If you have a credit card with nothing owed on the balance it may be advisable to go against mainstream advice and actually keep it for use later! This one seems strange, I know, but an empty credit card can make the difference if you are facing imminent hunger.

Do not use your credit card until such time that all of your cash flow dries up. This means all income from work, social welfare payments or money derived from selling your possessions. The credit card should be the very last thing used, as it is important to avoid monthly charges for as long as possible. When the time comes, begin using your credit card for emergency purchases only. These include food... that's it really, just food. By this stage, your finances will be in such a terrifying state that any and all luxuries will need to put aside in favour of the most basic of survival.

When the monthly bill arrives just withdraw cash from an ATM, using the credit card, to pay the minimum required. If you are extremely careful with your credit card use this system of withdrawing money from the credit card, to pay the credit card, could last several months. Be warned, that the amount of cash you are allowed to withdraw from the card is only a percentage of your available credit.

While this period of several months may be the time when your finances begin to improve it may also just be the end of everything you know. Homelessness may be beckoning. If you find that there is no imminent improvement in your financial situation where you are losing the house and about to end up homeless, this will be the time to use your credit card to purchase survival equipment for living on the street, such as sleeping bag, warm clothing and non-perishable foods.

If you do default on the credit card debt it may take several months for your bank to cancel the card and hand over your debt to a collection agency. Should this happen it may be possible to negotiate with the collection agency as they will have purchased your debt from the bank for far less than you owe. Let's say that you owe €10,000 on the credit card. The collection agency would have bought this debt for maybe... €700. They will, of course, attempt to collect the entire €10,000 owed but if you can show them an empty house and explain to them that you have nothing they suddenly become negotiable on the debt. Try to offer them €1,000 in cash to settle the account. This will represent a profit of €300 for the collection agency but you will need to come up with this €1,000 in cash within 1 or 2 hours. It is far easier to beg, borrow or steal €1,000 than €10,000 with family and friends being far more willing to help at this stage.

Healthcare

"The road to health is paved with good intestines!"
                    Sherry A. Rogers

In most countries, health care is extremely expensive and is usually covered by your employer but if you have recently lost your job it will be a very expensive prospect should you fall ill or get into an accident. It will now be your responsibility to ensure that you are as fit and healthy as possible. Just one trip to the doctor's office could cost so much that it may see you going without food for several days or luxuries like home heating or the use of electricity.

You don't need to splash out a small fortune on a gym membership or buy the most expensive organic foods. With just a few daily exercise routines it is possible to remain in reasonable enough health to avoid chronic illness. One of the biggest causes of disease and general ill health is stress. If you can keep yourself occupied and continue to boost your overall mood it will eliminate most of the stress that will be ever-present during times of crippling poverty.

While your, currently disastrous, financial situation might mean that nutritious or healthy food is no longer an option it is perfectly possible to survive on what you consider inferior food. The human body is one of the most adaptable species on this planet. We can survive in freezing arctic conditions just as easily as in desert regions. If we were a tropical fish, a change in environmental conditions by just 5°C (41°F) would be enough to kill us.

As long as you are able to stay clear of eating sweets all day, your body should be able to adapt to the move from healthy food to sub-par processed foodstuffs. Don't fall into the trap of a sedentary lifestyle and keep moving. Daily exercise is more important now than ever before.

Go outside

During times of extreme poverty, it is very easy to fall into a rut of staying at home, spending your days in front of the TV. If you have lost your job and are struggling to make ends meet the idea of going outside becomes an anxiety riddled nightmare of potential expense. You can't go to a fancy restaurant or for a few drinks in the evening with friends because it will cost far too much.

It is very important to get yourself off the sofa and go outside. The fresh air will do wonders for your overall mood and doesn't have to cost a fortune. Get into the habit of replacing nights out with friends, with a coffee and a chat instead. Meet your friends in a coffee shop of your choosing and just enjoy their company. You should be the one to select where you meet-up because you are the one struggling for money. If you don't, you may find yourself paying €5 or more for a mug of coffee. By selecting where to go, you are in control of the potential expense involved. There may be a nice, family run café nearby that provides teas and coffee at a reasonable price.

Social interaction is a necessary component of maintaining good mental health. Human beings are social creatures that rely on each other's company for protection and effective brain function. We are intimately tied together in a reciprocal relationship that requires us to interact regularly with each other. If you don't have any friends, this is your opportunity to find some. Just go outside and interact as much as possible. Eventually, you may meet someone who will become a great friend.

One of the cheapest ways to interact with friends is to invite them to your house for coffee and biscuits but don't neglect the importance of going outside. Once you're finished enjoying coffee at your house, bring them outside for a walk around the block while you talk to each other. If you can go outside, and interact with people, for just 30 minutes every 2 days it will be enough to keep your mood in high spirits.

Exercise

I know it might be hard to get some time, or even motivate yourself, into getting some exercise but keeping fit is more important now than ever before. To avoid dramatic healthcare bills or ongoing costs from medications you will need to get as fit as possible, as quickly as possible. The biggest problem with getting fit very quickly is that you could easily do damage to yourself, requiring the expensive healthcare system that you are trying to avoid.

You do not need to spend a fortune on a gym or personal trainer. If you are currently a gym member, cancel your account immediately and talk to the gym management about your current situation to see if you could get a partial refund. They will try to sell you slightly cheaper packages and generally do everything they can to make you stay, so be strong and stick to your guns. You can no longer afford this luxury and it must go. Be careful though, depending on your contract it may end up costing you more money to leave the gym than to stay. Check your contract very carefully before cancelling your membership.

Your daily exercise can be as simple as jogging around the block for 30 minutes each day for 5 or 6 days per week. This could be enough to keep you in reasonable shape. Apart from keeping you in shape, exercise has the added benefit of activating the reward centre of your brain which will deliver Serotonin (the feel good drug) throughout your system. This will have the immediate effect of boosting your mood, which is vital when facing crippling poverty.

The best time of day to exercise is first thing in the morning, if possible, as the release of Serotonin will continue for many hours afterwards. This boost in mood will literally keep you happy, optimistic and confident that everything will work out okay for your future. With such a boost in overall mood, you will be able to focus efficiently and effectively on your daily tasks.

If you decide to lift weights at home, on your own, you run the risk of being trapped under a heavy weight. Such accidents can land you in a hospital or at the worst result in your death. Remember, you can't afford a trip to the hospital right now so always perform weight training with a spotter.

Meditation

Being poor can, and will, generate huge levels of stress and anxiety which are detrimental to your overall health and well-being. Daily meditation exercises can alleviate stress and has a dramatic calming effect on the mind. Some of the most successful and prosperous people have incorporated meditation into their daily routines and many have attributed their great success in life to adopting this practice. When trapped in the cycle of crippling poverty, bear in mind that some of these prosperous figures were once where you are now, with some of them spending a year or more living rough.

Daily meditation does not need to consume most of your day and, in fact, should be limited to between 10-20 minutes. Meditation is the simple act of making yourself comfortable while simultaneously emptying your conscious mind of all thoughts. It is best if you can set aside a specific period each day, such as 30 minutes in the morning or evening, where you will spend 10-15 minutes preparing and the following 10-15 minutes actually meditating.

Before you begin ensure that all electronic devices are switched off... yes, that also means your phone. Any and all disturbances should be kept to a minimum during your meditation period. Either sit or lie down in a comfortable position and loosen or remove any restrictive clothing so that your mind is not going to focus on pain or pressure from them.

Close your eyes and simply listen to the sound of your own breathing. As your mind begins to wonder to various different thoughts, and it will, simply imagine each thought being trapped in a bubble and allow those bubbles to pop one at a time, thus removing these thoughts from existence. Concentrate on the sound of your own breathing and take deep measured breaths. That's all there is to it, empty your mind and listen to the sound of your breathing.

Employment costs money

"When you are unemployed, weekends are seven days long."
Mokokoma Mokhonoana

If you are unemployed and desperately searching for a job it can be very tempting to accept any offer that comes along but this could ultimately end up being a bad decision. While you will be receiving far more money each month you will lose all state benefits such as social welfare payments, childcare assistance, rent allowance and everything else that you were previously receiving. You will also need to pay travel expenses getting to and from work each day.

Depending on where you live, you may be receiving government healthcare assistance or any number of other benefits. You will need to calculate the value of everything that unemployment assistance is paying for in order to determine if a job offer will pay the same or more. It is possible to take up full-time employment and go even deeper into poverty as a result.

It is best to limit your search for work to within walking or cycling distance of your home. Don't just apply for those types of jobs you previously worked at or what your qualifications suggest but apply to absolutely everything available. If you are unsuccessful then expand the search distance to include every business and shop along your nearest bus or subway routes. By doing this it will cut down on travel costs as much as possible. Even if you own a car there is no point spending €40+ on fuel each week when you could spend under €10. The savings made on travel expenses can go towards paying off debts, buying yearly consumables or just for topping-up your savings account.

Preparing for the worst

"I was planning on my future as a homeless person. I had a really good spot picked out."
Larry David (1947-)

It's normal when you lose your job and begin the process of going broke to think that things can't possibly get any worse when suddenly even more crap falls on your shoulders. The final stage of crippling poverty, which is the stage that most people never reach, is homelessness. If you are lucky enough to see this impending disaster ahead of time it is possible to prepare in advance by purchasing some survival equipment, such as:

- Sleeping bag
- Ground mat
- Backpack
- Warm blankets
- Batteries
- Flashlight
- Matches
- Candles
- Underwear & socks

- Zip-lock or waterproof bags
- Deodorant
- Toilet paper
- Sewing kit
- Compact Toothbrush & toothpaste
- Medical supplies
- Wet wipes
- MRE's (Meals Ready to Eat)
- Nail clippers
- Anti-diarrhoea tablets
- Can opener
- Multi-tool
- Clothing
- Hat, scarf & gloves
- Good quality hiking boots
- Wind-up radio
- Compact solar charger

You will have a lot to carry so be sure to get every item in its most compact form possible. There will be no safe area to leave any of your possessions because they may be stolen or interfered with. Pack everything in such a way that the items most used are at the top of your backpack. This will minimise the amount of digging needed to reach something. Be sure to wrap all clothing and electronic items to ensure they don't succumb to wetness from a rain shower. Some backpacks will provide hooks and clips to attach additional smaller bags and containers on the outside. Utilise these hooks as much as possible for items that are regularly used.

Just because you are homeless does not mean that your identity has vanished. Important documents like birth certificate, passport or driver's licence must be kept safe at all times. Envelopes designed for photographs can help as they contain a strong cardboard inlay to prevent bending. Ensure that this protective envelope has a closable flap that can be resealed, such as button clips or one with a string that can be wrapped around a metal clasp.

Join a local church

Given the charitable nature of religious organisations, joining one can benefit you greatly when preparing for homelessness. It doesn't matter if you believe in a religion or not, what matters most is the help and assistance that they could provide. If things have got so bad that you are barely holding onto your house while regularly starving yourself in order to get the mortgage company off your back, a local church offers the potential for free food, some financial assistance and generating useful contacts.

In some countries, Sunday mass also includes a meal afterwards for the congregation. It is normal in these circumstances that parishioners will bring a dish and everyone will share, similar to a potluck dinner. Arriving without food will quickly show everyone else that you are struggling and as you shovel down your meal they may discuss your situation amongst themselves. If you are pleasant and approachable, as a general rule, they may offer more assistance than just a free meal, but this cannot be guaranteed.

While food and shelter could be provided by the church and fellow parishioners you may not receive any cash. This is understandable as they may have been burned in the past by unscrupulous people who tried to extort money from them, or they simply may not have it to give. Take anything that they offer, as a refusal could quickly put a stop to any further assistance.

The most valuable resource that can be received from joining a local church group is the contacts available. Everyone who regularly attends mass will most likely look after each other just like any other tight-knit group. Somebody may own a business and require an employee or they could assist with a job search. You will need to talk to as many people as possible in order to get the message out there that you are desperately in need of employment and are willing to work hard.

Find emergency services

Don't wait until you are actually homeless to seek out the services you will need on a daily basis. Begin researching your local area to find food banks and places where homeless people gather in the evenings to receive a meal from mobile food stations.

Where do your local homeless population sleep at night? Check these areas to see if they are safe places to be... they're usually not. Seek out suitable alternative places and monitor them for a few nights in a row to see if other people are going there, passing through the area or if there is any activity whatsoever.

If doctors and hospitals are not free in your country, region or city, where do homeless people go when they get sick or injured? It is far more difficult to find these places when you are homeless and injured. Take note of them, what services they can offer and when they are open.

Emergency accommodation, for the homeless, vulnerable or those escaping domestic violence may not be the most desirable places to stay. Crime and violence seem to permeate these places, with many homeless people opting to sleep on the street rather than risking their lives and property in emergency accommodation. Avoid government controlled homeless shelters at all costs, unless the weather conditions are so treacherous as to demand staying in these shelters, so you don't die from exposure by staying outside.

One of the best resources for discovering such services are the homeless people themselves. Talk to them; find out where they go, what they can get on a daily basis and what areas of the city are safe to sleep at night. Even though you may be desperately poor, always reward a homeless person if they give you vital information. Give them some money or cigarettes. Such generosity will be returned to you in the future.

Living in your car

If you do end up homeless yet still have your own car, it is possible to live successfully whilst avoiding much of the dangers of living rough. The biggest problem with living in your car is that it is illegal in most countries, with heavy fines imposed if you are caught. If you can see homelessness on the horizon, long before losing your home, consider trading in your current vehicle for a van. It might seem tempting to buy a purpose built luxury camper but these tend to cost a lot more to run than a small delivery van.

The best type to get is a windowless delivery van as these will offer concealment when sleeping. A camper van will immediately attract attention if you are parked anywhere but a trailer park or camping spot.

You will need to have amenities close by, such as toilets and showers. If you still have a gym membership that hasn't expired yet you can avail of their facilities. Some colleges and universities take a fairly lax approach when it comes to checking ID's at their gym facilities and sports arenas. Take full advantage of such oversight by discretely slipping in to use the showers and toilets. If you have difficulties finding facilities to maintain good hygiene try to locate a swimming pool that does not require membership. Most of these places will charge up to €10 to use the swimming pool. If you can afford this once per week it is possible to have a basic level of overall hygiene while using wet wipes, to wash with, during the remaining weekdays.

You will need to have an address in order to pay road tax, insurance or renew your driving licence. Try to find a family member or friend who will allow you to use their address but if this is not possible, set up a post box before you lose your home.

Securing your vehicle becomes even more important now because if your car is stolen, so is your home. If you don't have an alarm system installed, get this done before moving into your car. Buy a steering lock and use it anytime you are away from home (your car).

When searching for a location to park make use of 24-hour stores with parking lots. Large chain stores should have ample parking available and will usually have toilet facilities for customers. Church parking lots can, in most cases, be used for overnight parking but always select a new location each night so that you don't draw unwanted attention to yourself.

Large marinas offer some of the best parking places as they usually cater to sailors, who park their vehicles there for weeks at a time and provide shower facilities and rest areas. This is also a good place to find temporary work that pays in cash.

Dangers of homelessness

Being homeless puts you in a vulnerable position filled with many dangers. When you are homeless it will inevitably make you a target by people who view you as the lowest form of creature on Earth, and there are a lot of people who think this way. In some countries, the danger of harassment or bullying comes from the very people sworn to protect you... the police. Some of them will use their power of authority to intimidate, harass, assault and even torture some homeless people who fall within their jurisdiction or patrol route. City councils have also begun to harass the homeless with the introduction of by-laws which impose hefty fines for simply being homeless. These fines will continue to mount up until the ultimate arrest and detention of these vulnerable individuals.

Be very careful who you accept help from when sleeping rough as you can become prey to serial killers and rapists. The reason for targeting the homeless is because it is far less likely that someone is looking for that person, will put pressure on the police to find them or spark off a quick investigation due to the victim not showing up for work, etc. It may seem that being invisible will keep you safe but this will only put you in a position where you can be preyed upon more easily. If you are sleeping in a dark alley, and nobody knows you are there, your potential attack may go unnoticed. Stay in the open and remain with, or near, as many people as possible. Some homeless people prefer to stay in tight-knit groups for protection and will maintain a watch schedule so that one of them will always be awake to alert the others of danger.

In some instances, homeless people have been discovered with full-time jobs but due to their vulnerability were either not paid or supplied with a basic meal for a full day's work. While living on the streets you will become prey to those who have no problem with using and abusing you.

Cold weather will be one of the most dangerous times for anyone sleeping rough. Not only could you freeze to death but you are also at risk from colds and flu associated with winter conditions. Hypothermia can set in very quickly and result in death within 15 minutes of the first symptoms. After food and water, keeping warm should be your highest priority during the winter months with preparations being made during the summer. Seek out warm clothes and anything that could provide heat.

Shoplifting

Shoplifting, as we all know, is a crime but when you are faced with the prospect of starving to death it will become necessary to break the law in order to survive. This one will depend entirely on where in the world you live as shoplifting can attract extremely harsh penalties in some countries.

When stealing from a shop it is important to only take items that you desperately need for immediate survival, such as food or water. Even stealing a bottle of soda is unacceptable as this will be considered a luxury item if you are caught in the act.

During the aftermath of hurricane Katrina in 2005 there were large numbers of looting incidents, where people were arrested, and in some cases shot by police officers. The only exceptions were people stealing food, water and nappies. These people were usually allowed to go free with their stolen items.

There have been plenty of cases across the world where starving homeless people have been caught shoplifting only to have the police buy them some food before letting them go free. This cannot be relied upon and you should expect a penalty if found with stolen items. The decision to steal will be yours to make but will most likely be guided by unquenchable starvation. Make your decisions wisely and always keep in mind that you are only doing this to survive. Your life is far more important than any punishments that could come your way.

If you can prove that shoplifting is the only way to stave off starvation you may be treated leniently in the eyes of the law. This is only a maybe, you could also end up in jail but if you are already at the point of starvation jail will ensure that you receive food on a daily basis.

A brighter future?

"Keep looking up! I learn from the past, dream about the future and look up. There's nothing like a beautiful sunset to end a healthy day."
Rachel Boston (1982-)

Poverty is a result of simply lacking enough money. Given unlimited resources would you really choose to go hungry or go without those things you need or want? The poverty trap you are currently embroiled in is temporary. You must spend your time in the firm and unwavering belief that this situation will change. But what happens when your finances do improve?

It may be tempting to immediately get stuck into spending your hard-earned wages each month but always remember that this kind of rampant spending was probably the reason for your poverty in the first place. Stay strong and remember that a healthy balance of savings will ensure that future hiccups in your financial situation will be easy to deal with. The absolute minimum to save each week, or month, is 10% of your take home pay. Everything else can go on rent or mortgage repayments, food, travel and entertainment.

To plan for financial freedom it is advisable to keep living as you did while you were poor. Don't waste money on wild nights out, instead make this a once every month or once every two months occasion, with the intervening nights out being ones where you drive to the pub and enjoy a few sodas. Stop getting takeaway food every night of the week and continue to grow your own food in the back garden.

If you are able to cut your spending enough it may take only a few years to save enough money to fully pay off your mortgage or allow for a comfortable retirement.

You could also save for future living expenses. Let's say that you are 50 years old and will live till maybe... 70. This means that you will need to save enough money to allow for a basic level of survival for 20 years. If your current weekly expenses, for basic survival supplies such as food and toiletries, are €40 you will need to save

€41,600. If you scrimp and save for the next 5 years it will cost you around €693, from your paycheck each month to realise this goal. Once this amount is saved, you will never need to worry about starving to death during any future financial troubles.

Everything that you can save after this basic amount will be a bonus. You can begin saving for holidays, entertainment or to pay off the mortgage early. The more you can save for your future, right now, the better your future will be.

Never give up

It doesn't matter what struggles come your way in the future, what matters most is that you never give up on your dreams and goals. Never allow doubts or fears to cloud your judgment as you strive forward, as these will only slow you down.

Not only should you never give up when faced with financial obstacles that are in the way of your work, personal life or success but also when faced with obstacles in your mind that may be preventing you from moving forward. Fears and doubts will fester and grow but only if you allow them to.

If you firmly believe that **you will succeed**, no matter how difficult the future may seem or how much work could be involved then you will be successful eventually. If you don't believe in yourself then you can't possibly achieve anything you set your mind to. The belief in yourself can be so powerful that it will begin to change your circumstances if you let it. If you are going through financial difficulties, instead of believing that this is just your lot in life it is far better if you **firmly believe** that you are perfectly fine and everything will work out for your benefit. Do not give the financial troubles any space in your mind or allow it to kill your future dreams or goals.

You will face many obstacles in life but remember, as you strive towards your goals, that these obstacles can and will be overcome. In this world or instant gratification, it is those who realise that things take time and effort are the ones who usually succeed and enjoy the riches of success. Things don't happen instantly but if you persevere, with an unwavering belief that **you can succeed** then you will succeed.

Always believe in yourself because, at the end of the day, you are the only one who truly cares. The most important thing is that **things will happen for you** if you just believe. Never give up; it's such a wonderful life.

Remember to give back

During your time of financial distress, you were more than likely helped by many people or organisations. It is very important to reward this help as soon as you can. You can reward family and friends by refunding any money they gave you or by treating them to fancy meals, nights out on the town or presents. Some people may demand that you pay them back. If a family member or friend is badly harassing you for the return of, what was clearly charity at the time, you have two choices; pay them first or pay them last. Some people find it only fitting to pay them last because of the level of harassment levied on them and others will prefer to pay them first so that the negative energy of such harassment is removed as early as possible. This choice will be yours and yours alone.

Many food banks, homeless charities and other organisations may have been providing assistance to you which should also be repaid. Donate supplies, food, or money. You could even volunteer by joining the organisation and helping other poor people.

The reason for giving back when you can is to keep your Karma clear. If you don't it is possible that this could be seen as greed which will, in turn, bite you sometime in the future. Besides, it's nice to be nice. You were helped during your time of need and it is only right to give back, now that you can.

Conclusion

"We are not rich by what we possess but by what we can do without."
  Immanuel Kant (1724-1804)

As you have seen, from your experiences with crippling poverty, it is possible to survive. As you strive forward remember to live within your means and never allow your spending to get out of control ever again. You don't need to have the latest items and certainly don't need to *"keep up with the Jones's"*. Always, and only, buy what works for you and never allow yourself to be influenced by the spending habits of others.

The most important thing in life is to survive, to put food on the table and be able to warm your home. Everything after that should be considered a bonus.

Don't forget to be grateful for everything in your life, no matter how small and stay positive always. I wish you all the best in your attempts to turn a bad financial situation into a great one and know that **you can do it**.

About Tadhg O'Flaherty

As a computer whizz-kid, Tadhg was naturally inept at writing until he discovered that by utilising the Law of Attraction he was able to seamlessly transition into the field and is now a full-time author with several books currently self-published on Amazon.

Tadhg's second book "Surviving a Realistic Zombie Apocalypse" gained local notoriety within days of publishing and was featured on the front page of the Limerick Leader newspaper, which has a readership of 110,290 and also received airtime on local and national radio.

To find out more, visit Tadhg's website and sign up to the author's mailing list for advanced notice of new releases, promotions and more.

www.tadhgfla.com

Author's Note

Thank you for reading "**Surviving Crippling Poverty**". I hope you enjoyed this book. Word-of-mouth is vital for the success of any author. Please consider leaving a review on Amazon. Each review makes all the difference and would be greatly appreciated.

Also by Tadhg O'Flaherty

How to Get Over Her in 1 Month: Learn how to rise like a Phoenix from the ashes of a breakup

Surviving a Realistic Zombie Apocalypse

Prepper's: The Ultimate Guide

Living Off-Grid

Living a Happy Life

Living a Productive Life

Do You Really Exist?

How to Reprogram Your Subconscious

www.ingramcontent.com/pod-product-compliance
Lightning Source LLC
Chambersburg PA
CBHW030741180526
45163CB00003B/874

9781520583945